# Bhagavad Gita on
# Effective Leadership

# Bhagavad Gita on Effective Leadership

◆

## Timeless Wisdom for Leaders

*Pujan Roka*

iUniverse, Inc.
New York  Lincoln  Shanghai

# Bhagavad Gita on Effective Leadership
## Timeless Wisdom for Leaders

iUniverse books may be ordered through booksellers or by contacting:

iUniverse
2021 Pine Lake Road, Suite 100
Lincoln, NE 68512
www.iuniverse.com
1-800-Authors (1-800-288-4677)

ISBN-13: 978-0-595-37040-5 (pbk)
ISBN-13: 978-0-595-67447-3 (cloth)
ISBN-13: 978-0-595-81444-2 (ebk)
ISBN-10: 0-595-37040-3 (pbk)
ISBN-10: 0-595-67447-X (cloth)
ISBN-10: 0-595-81444-1 (ebk)

Printed in the United States of America

In memory of my loving father, Dr. R. K. Roka

# Contents

In these times of unprecedented global stresses, leaders of all sorts need to achieve deeper levels of clarity and connection (with nature and their higher selves) than traditionally required in order to "do business as usual." So, it is not surprising that many are renewing serious study of ancient wisdom traditions of all sorts, including timeless texts like the Bhagavad Gita. Both ancient and modern wisdom still come down to wisdom, the most precious commodity in all times of profound change.

**Peter Senge**
Best-selling author of *The Fifth Discipline*

# *Note on Textual Citations*

References to verses of the Bhagavad Gita are represented in the form of chapter and verse after quotations, with Bhagavad Gita omitted from the parenthetical citation. For example, verse 7 of chapter 1 is represented as 1:7. A sequence of verses, such as verses seven through nine of chapter 1, would be represented in the text as 1:7–9.

All other citations appear in Notes and References.

# Preface

When I was introduced to the Bhagavad Gita several years ago, I was fascinated with its poetic verses and its philosophical teachings. I started looking at the Bhagavad Gita in a different perspective when I started exploring the subject of leadership as part of my academic and professional pursuits. I noticed many remarkable leadership lessons embedded within the Gita.

The Bhagavad Gita is predominantly considered as a work of ancient wisdom. It has been widely studied in the contexts of philosophy, theology, and ancient Eastern literature. However, the Bhagavad Gita is yet to be explored in the context of leadership. *Bhagavad Gita on Effective Leadership* is an attempt to study its discourses in the leadership context.

Many contemporary writers and thinkers of leadership have presented concepts, theories, or practices that are similar to the concepts discussed in the Bhagavad Gita, however, there is no literature that compares the concepts discussed in the Bhagavad Gita with present-day concepts and practices. In this book, I have focused on the relevance of the Bhagavad Gita with contemporary leadership theories and practices.

I do not expect every reader of this book to be a master in the subject of leadership, or the Bhagavad Gita. Leadership is a universal topic and every one of us is affected by it in one way or the other. Today, we understand leadership as a topic that is not only about leading a nation, a corporation, or a big entity, but is about influencing and guiding others. It is about showing the direction by ideas and actions.

To those who have never been exposed to the Bhagavad Gita, I have included the key and relevant verses in each chapter. To those who are well versed with the Gita, this book is not a verse-by-verse translation. I have taken only key verses that are relevant to the topic of leadership.

Chapters and verses in this book are in the same sequence as in the original Bhagavad Gita. Some of the concepts are repeated several times in the Bhagavad Gita. I have tried to explore different contexts behind the same concepts that appear in multiple places in the original text.

Pujan Roka
April 2005

# Introduction

Many stories and historical texts of the ancient Indian subcontinent present accounts of countries filled with brave and intelligent leaders who led vibrant kingdoms that had rich palaces and cities, and big forts and armies. The ancient Indian subcontinent, as we know from these stories and accounts, was a thriving civilization. Ancient temples, palaces, forts, and pagodas, many of which have endured their original structure, provide a hint at the thriving civilization that existed thousands of years ago. Growing up in the ancient city of Kathmandu, Nepal, I used to look at the ancient temples, palaces, courts, and pagodas and wondered how people in those times were able to build such structures that were rich in beauty and architecture. In ancient times, Kathmandu was a city that thrived in trade and commerce. It had business links with many other places in Asia. Several other places in the region witnessed similar prosperity during those times. Rich in architecture, trade, commerce, and other traditions, this ancient civilization was only possible with effective leadership.

What was the basis of leadership in the Indian subcontinent during those ancient times? Formal writings on leadership were not available—not at least to the knowledge of the modern world. The only available literatures were the ancient scriptures such as the *Vedas* and the *Upanishads*. One of the scriptures was the Bhagavad Gita—known as "the sacred song of God"—considered by many as the scripture that summarized the essence of ancient Eastern teachings and wisdom. The Bhagavad Gita presents the dialogue between two prominent leaders—*Lord Krishna* and the warrior prince *Arjuna*—before the battle of *Kurukshetra* in the epic of *Mahabharata*. Mahabharata is the epic of the feud between two clans of a royal family, namely the virtuous *Pandavas* and the wicked *Kauravas*. The army of the Pandavas is led by Arjuna[1] and the army of the Kauravas is led by *Bheesma*. Before the start of the battle of Kurushetra, Arjuna requests his charioteer, Krishna, who is also his friend, mentor, and a godly incarnation, to drive the chariot to the middle of the battlefield, so he can observe both armies.

As Arjuna observes his own family members and kinsmen standing on the opposite sides of the battlefield, he fears fighting this battle. He laments to his charioteer that he has no interest to fight against his own kinsmen. Seeing a close friend and a warrior lament, Krishna counsels Arjuna, "Nothing is higher than a war against evil. A warrior such as you should be pleased when faced with such a war, as it leads to heaven" (2:32–33). Krishna's discourses are described in the eighteen chapters of the Bhagavad Gita. At the end of the discourses, Krishna successfully convinces Arjuna to pick up his bow and arrow, and fight the battle of Kurukshetra. The episodes leading to the battle and the aftermath are described in the epic of Mahabharata.

It is not known when exactly the Bhagavad Gita was written. Some scholars have speculated that it was written in as early as 3000 BC. Through these thousands of years, the Bhagavad Gita has endured as a revered text of ancient wisdom. It has endured as a masterpiece in the world of literature. To the Hindus, it has endured as a timeless scripture with discourses from Krishna—the godly incarnation. The original Sanskrit text of the Bhagavad Gita has been translated in many languages. Scholars like Ralph Emerson, Henry D. Thoreau, and T. S. Eliot have studied the Gita with great interest. They have quoted the Gita in many of their writings. Contemporary management thinkers like Peter Senge have also quoted the Gita in their writings.[2]

---

**Famous Scholars on Bhagavad Gita**

*When I read the Bhagavad-Gita and reflect about how God created this universe everything else seems so superfluous.* [3]
—Albert Einstein

*I owed a magnificent day to the Bhagavat-Gita. It was the first of books; it was as if an empire spoke to us, nothing small or*

*unworthy, but large, serene, consistent, the voice of an old intelligence which in another age and climate had pondered and thus disposed of the same questions that exercise us.* [4]
—Ralph Waldo Emerson

*In the morning I bathe my intellect in the stupendous and cosmogonal philosophy of the Bhagvat-Geeta, since whose composition years of the gods have elapsed, and in comparison with which our modern world and its literature seem puny and trivial; and I doubt if that philosophy is not to be referred to a previous state of existence, so remote is its sublimity from our conceptions.* [5]
—Henry David Thoreau

In the Indian subcontinent, the Bhagavad Gita has been a subject of faith and strength to many leaders, most notably to Mahatma Gandhi. "Man is not at peace with himself till he has become like unto God," said Gandhi in a 1931 issue of *Young India*. "The endeavor to reach this state is the supreme, the only ambition worth having. And this is self-realization. This self-realization is the subject of the Gita."

Leaders like Gandhi and many scholars throughout the ages have considered the Bhagavad Gita as a practical guide to living a meaningful and fulfilling life. They have revered the Gita as a guide to self-realization and the attainment of the highest spiritual state. Broadly speaking, anyone can apply the teachings of the Gita in his or her life. If we look closely, the Gita is also a source of great lessons on leadership. For instance, the Gita signifies Arjuna's journey of leadership when he is confronted with the challenges of a war. As a leader, he is faced with the challenges of leading his organization—the clan of the Pandavas. The teachings of Krishna transform Arjuna in embarking on that leadership journey and take up the challenges of a leader.

The teachings of the Bhagavad Gita are largely considered spiritual teachings. Contemporary leadership based on spirituality and faith is not new to the world. Prominent thinkers and writers in leadership like

H. Dale Burke, John H. Maxwell, Laurie Beth Jones, Andy Stanley, and many others have been influenced by their spirituality and faith-based backgrounds. Jimmy Carter, the thirty-ninth President of the United States, has written extensively about spirituality and its association with leadership. All of their writings signify that there is a lot about leadership to be learned from spirituality and faith.

The leadership lessons derived from spirituality and faith encompass the age old values and virtues such as vision, excellence, integrity, perseverance, and discipline, which are also applicable to the contemporary leadership scenarios. These values and virtues are the pillars of leadership in any group, place, or time.

It is also noteworthy here to mention that the concept of Spiritual Intelligence, also known as SQ, is becoming popular in organizational and leadership development. A concept made widely popular by writers like Danah Zohar, Ian Marshall, and Richard Wolman, SQ is our access to and use of meaning, vision and value in the way that we think and the decisions we make. It is the ultimate intelligence of the human beings—the intelligence of the spirit, the intelligence of the soul. [6] The core characteristics of SQ, such as self-awareness, vision, and values, are very relevant to the needs of contemporary leadership. Hence, spirituality and leadership come together in terms of their fundamental values.

Today, the emergence of spiritual leadership has also been widely accepted by the leading authorities in the field of leadership. Spiritual leadership is not necessarily related to a specific spirituality, religion, or tradition. Rather, it involves motivating people by influencing their souls or spirit instead of controlling them. In the new age, leaders must acknowledge this as an important aspect of leadership.

# 1

## *The Leadership Challenges*

# Call for Leadership

The opening chapter of the Bhagavad Gita presents the powerful imagery of the battlefield of Kurukshetra where the armies of the Pandavas and the Kauravas faced each other in combat. Arjuna leads the army of the Pandavas, and Bheesma leads the army of the Kauravas. Both armies are decorated with formidable warriors. As they line up against their enemies in the battlefield, they blow their conches and trumpets and beat their drums to signal their preparedness for the battle.

Before the battle starts, Arjuna asks his charioteer, Lord Krishna, to take his chariot between the two armies, so he can observe his enemies. As Arjuna notices close family members and kinsmen line up to fight against him, he trembles at the thought of killing them in combat. "Oh Krishna," he laments, "I have no desire to fight this battle. I have no desire for victory or the pleasure of a kingdom.... I have no desire to fight against my kinsmen, even if it means a place in heaven" (1:32, 1:35).

The opening chapter not only begins a dialogue between the despairing warrior Arjuna and the godly incarnation Krishna, but it also sets the stage for a leadership call for Arjuna. As mentioned in the introduction, Arjuna has already played various leadership roles before the account of the Bhagavad Gita. Krishna's discourses are aimed at enlightening Arjuna to accept his new leadership role in the battle of Kurukshetra. Thousands of years later, we can now relate this as *situational leadership*—a leader's ability to read each situation and to adapt accordingly.

# Accountability

It is important to note that the context of war in the Bhagavad Gita is not necessarily directed to violence and bloodshed. The chapter's core message centers on how a leader manages conflicts and adversity. Many scholars of the Bhagavad Gita have described this chapter as the conflict that brews in people's minds. Leaders bear the highest level of accountability in an organization. When conflicts and adversity overshadow an organization, its leader is responsible for the consequences of those problems. Arjuna's grievances suggest that he acknowledged his responsibility as the leader of the Pandavas' army.

The conflict between the Pandavas and the Kauravas is basically a family feud. Mostly influenced by the malicious brother Duryodhana, the Kauravas want to drive the Pandavas away from their kingdom, so they can reign with absolute authority. First, they attempt to kill the Pandavas by setting their palace on fire. Later, the Kauravas fool the Pandavas in a wager that forces them to leave the kingdom for thirteen years. After the thirteenth year, Duryodhana's refusal to share the kingdom with the Pandavas leads to the battle of Kurukshetra. (The details of these accounts are described in the epic of Mahabharata.)

The Kauravas initiated the conflict with the Pandavas for their own selfish desires. The Kauravas are less interested in the future state of their families and kingdom, which need the able leadership of the more benevolent Pandavas. The Kauravas are less effective leaders; their only philosophy is to lead by malice and terror.

Opposed to the philosophy of the Kauravas, Arjuna shows compassion at the time of war. His love toward his family members remains undeterred although they stand on the opposite side of the battlefield. "When a family is destroyed, the family values and traditions are also destroyed," laments Arjuna as Krishna stills the chariot in the middle of the battlefield. "The destruction of the family values and traditions leads to the destruction of society" (1:40–41).

## Organizational Cultures and Values

Like Arjuna, an effective leader is always cognizant of cultures, values, and traditions—factors of any organization. When faced with adversity, a leader must use these factors or reference points to analyze problems and to guide the organization while preserving its essence.

The emphasis on organizational culture is not to maintain its status quo but to identify its positive and negative aspects. Positive aspects of the culture must be preserved while negative ones must be eliminated. The negative cultural aspects Arjuna faces are the Kauravas' malicious intention to break apart and disrupt the family and the kingdom. In the battle of Kurukshetra, the Kauravas are aided by stout warriors who are kinsmen to both clans. Arjuna is faced with the moral dilemma of fighting against his kinsmen on the Kauravas' side and whether to end the association with his evil kinsmen and their aides-de-camp. The following chapters illustrate how Krishna helped Arjuna resolve his dilemma.

Organizational cultures and values have always been important to successful organizations, whether in Arjuna's times or in the modern world. For instance, former CEO of International Business Machines (IBM) Louis V. Gerstner Jr. found organizational culture to be a key ingredient to generate business value.[1] During the early 1990s, IBM was at the brink of a breakup. By preserving the positive aspects of the organizational culture and by eliminating its negative aspects, Gerstner successfully led the company through this time of trouble. By the end of his tenure, IBM had regained its business health. Arjuna's and Gerstner's experiences are similar with respect to organizational culture. Building an organization upon the positive aspects of culture was something Arjuna would learn later in Mahabharata, and it is what IBM learned from its near-death experience.

## Learning from Conflicts and Adversity

If many Vedic scholars have considered the Bhagavad Gita the essence of the Eastern scriptures, why does the topic of conflicts and adversity appear in the very first chapter? If Krishna is a godly incarnation, why are peace and tranquility not the opening message of the Bhagavad Gita? If Krishna had already saved people from many diabolical characters before, why is he unable to eradicate the Kauravas without war and conflict for the Pandavas?

Since the beginning of humankind, people have been a combative species. The human species has left no conflict untested. Territorial, racial, religious, and political conflicts are some of the broader categories of conflicts that have existed since prehistoric times. Conflicts and adversities are fundamental to human nature, and every generation has faced conflicts. But what do conflicts and adversity have to do with leadership?

Sooner or later, every leader must deal with adversity. Great leaders usually excel in times of great difficulty. Is the Bhagavad Gita suggesting that Arjuna needs to face adversity to become a more effective leader? It is through adversity that a person's or a leader's character is revealed. Great and effective leadership is impossible without character. Dr. Martin Luther King Jr. once said that the ultimate measure of a man is not where he stands in moments of comfort and convenience but where he stands during challenges and controversy.

We have seen several examples of this in our history. Mahatma Gandhi's nonviolent fight against the British Empire, Nelson Mandela's struggle against South African apartheid, and Dr. King's fight against racial segregation are a few of many examples of conflict and adversity that help build the character of leaders. A leader should learn from conflicts and adversity to become more effective.

## Chapter 1: Krishna's Leadership Lessons

- Leaders should embrace rather than avoid formidable challenges because they bring out the leaders' greatest strengths.

- It is crucial for leaders to distinguish the positive from the negative aspects of organizational culture to enhance the positive and eliminate the negative.

- Conflicts and adversities are leaders' best opportunities for learning and growing. Great leaders usually perform well in times of great conflict and adversity.

- The more one deals with problems and setbacks successfully, the more one becomes a true leader.

# 2

## *The Purpose of Leadership*

## Self-Awareness and Empathy

As Arjuna laments his dilemma of fighting the battle of Kurukshetra, Krishna tries to console him, "It is not wise for an intelligent being like you to lament at the time of crisis. You should not be weak at the time of adversity; you should fight the adversities with a brave heart" (2:2–3). Arjuna continues to grieve at the thought of killing his kinsmen in the battlefield. Krishna says, "You should not grieve for those who are not worthy to be grieved for. The wise grieve neither for the living nor for the dead" (2:11).

Here Krishna alludes to self-awareness and empathy, the key factors that determine a leader's effectiveness. Today, authorities in psychology have suggested that a leader's emotional intelligence, such as self-awareness and empathy, plays a key role in the overall performance of an organization.[1] A leader's emotional intelligence can induce a positive organizational culture. High levels of emotional intelligence create a culture that promotes information sharing, trust, and collaborative learning. Low levels of emotional intelligence create a culture full of doubts and distrust.

Self-awareness helps leaders grow accustomed to their guiding values. Leaders with higher levels of self-awareness assess their own strengths and weaknesses well. Since they can identify their strengths, they also tend to be confident in their actions.

Krishna's discourses focus on increasing Arjuna's confidence before the battle starts, requiring Arjuna to become aware of his emotions and encouraging him to channel them in positive ways. With this reflection, Arjuna could become cognizant of the proper course of action to resolve the crisis. Even before the battle of Kurukshetra, Arjuna was an accomplished warrior. He had a history of winning difficult battles. His combat skills were unquestionable, yet his anguish at the circumstances of the battle was likely to prevent him from reaching his full potential.

A weak leader can neither manage crises nor lead his or her organization. Arjuna's despair is bound to weaken him, reducing his effectiveness in fighting the war. Therefore, it is important for Arjuna to remain positive before the battle. It is important for Arjuna to be resilient in the time of crisis. As a friend, mentor, and charioteer, Krishna's responsibility is to encourage Arjuna, so the leader can alter his mindset in realistic terms with the conflict in hand.

Krishna also takes a hard stance at fighting against the causes of dissonance. A person or a group that causes internal rifts deserves no compassion in the eyes of leadership. Grieving over the elimination of dissidents does not help the organization. Krishna notes that since the Kauravas were antagonists toward the peace process, they deserve no compassion from Arjuna or the Pandavas.

Krishna also counsels that "the wise grieve neither for the living nor for the dead" (2:11). A leader should not delve too much into the past or in the present although he or she cannot ignore the lessons of the past and the day-to-day operations. A leader's main focus should be on guiding his team and organization toward the future and the strategies to attain his organization's goals.

## Leaving a Legacy

An effective leader's role spans much beyond the tenure he or she serves in an organization, and a leader can leave a legacy if his or her ideologies incorporate enduring values.

This kind of legacy is seen in many organizations, communities, and nations around the world. Gandhi's legacy of freedom in India, Dr. King's legacy in the civil rights movement in the United States, Tom Watson Sr.'s legacy of growth at IBM, Bill Hewlett and Dave Packard's legacy in Hewlett-Packard—all these are examples of leaders' legacies in their respective environments.

Krishna supports a supreme legacy for his friend and leader, Arjuna, when he says, "There has never been a time when you, I, and these kings have not existed, nor will there be a time when we will cease to exist" (2:12). Krishna stresses the immortality of leaders and their legacies on the earth. At a time of a great crisis, it is important for Arjuna to think of his legacy for his family, his kingdom, and the generations that would follow him.

"Breaking away from the selfish ego of *I, me,* and *mine* takes a person from death to immortality," says Krishna (2:71–72). According to the ancient Vedic tradition, the confinement of our mindset to physical existence limits our true potential, especially when a leader confines himself to his physical existence defined only in terms of *I, me,* and *mine.* This confinement dilutes the true potential of leadership. A leader's legacy is enhanced when he or she leads with the organization's interests foremost in mind. A leader who works toward the purpose of the common good is remembered even after his or her death, becoming immortal through the legacy left behind.

## Leader as Change Agent

Krishna consoles Arjuna about the impermanence of life and its matters: "The soul dwells in a body through childhood and old age and attains a new body after the death. The wise are not deluded by changes" (2:13). Krishna suggests that an effective leader should always be unfettered by the impermanence of life and the changes that are always present in this world. By acknowledging the impermanence of life, a leader should know that he or she is a change agent—someone who brings about the transformation of an organization, community, or a nation. Sometimes, one must sacrifice personal interests for that change, and sometimes, this cost might mean one's own life. However, a purpose-driven leader should not be fettered by the impermanence of life. The effective leader champions peace and growth, regardless of the potential changes that may lie ahead.

Why would a leader sacrifice his or her own life for a change? We could call this an extreme measure of leadership, but we do not have to go that far in history to collect stories of leaders who risked their own lives to bring about change and transformation to their organizations and causes. Their bold beliefs and values cost them their own lives. Countless leaders have had to place their lives at risk to bring about changes within their organizations or for their causes. Gandhi, Abraham Lincoln, Dr. King, Yitzhak Rabin—all these leaders were assassinated chiefly because of their beliefs and values.

In the business world, we see leaders who are willing to take maximum risk to bring about sweeping changes in their businesses. Former CEO of IBM Louis V. Gerstner Jr., former CEO of General Electric Jack Welch, and CEO of Cisco John Chambers are some of the business leaders who have become successful in creating enduring corporations through sweeping changes and transformations. Although these modern-day counterparts to past leaders did not have to sacrifice their own lives, they did endure great struggles in their own ways.

Leaders who accept the impermanence of life and changes develop into fearless leaders; that is, leaders who do not fear change. They become true change agents and transformational leaders.

## Resilience in Action

On December 22, 2003, the Green Bay Packers were about to play an important Monday night football game against the Oakland Raiders. Something was unusual about the Green Bay Packers that night. The Packers' quarterback Brett Favre's father had died the previous night. Everyone was surprised to see Favre on the field ready to take on the leadership role of a quarterback instead of being with his family. No one expected an extraordinary game from Favre who led the team to victory over the Raiders. People were surprised at his performance, and his resilience in winning the game despite his recent personal tragedy.

As Krishna continues to console and motivate Arjuna, he says, "Those who are not affected by the feelings of pain and pleasure are wise and fit for immortality" (2:15). In the context of leadership, the word *immortality* here alludes to leadership legacy. Although it is very difficult not to be affected by pain and pleasure, it is important for leaders to be resilient in their action and in their responsibilities to their organizations. Brett Favre's performance on that Monday night is an exemplar of effective leadership and resilience in action.

Managing pain and focusing on leadership simultaneously is very difficult, and doing the same for pleasure may be equally difficult. Sometimes, happiness, relaxation, and comfort hinder leaders from thinking seriously about the future. When Sam Palmisano took over as CEO of IBM in 2002, the former CEO Gerstner had already transformed IBM from its near-death experience to an enduring company. Palmisano was faced with the challenge of maintaining company growth. Palmisano believed that the company needed to be reenergized even when business was good. He came up with the idea of reinventing the company's values as a way to manage and grow business. By analyzing through surveys and focus groups, Palmisano implemented a revised set of new corporate values in 2003. [2] Some years have passed since then, and IBM is still growing bigger and stronger.

## Essence of Leadership

According to the Vedic tradition, the soul is the essence of self and mortal life. "The soul is never born; it never dies," says Krishna reinforcing the permanent nature of the soul (2:20). "The soul is eternal and indestructible, and it is not destroyed even after the end of the mortal life it inhabits in" (2:21).

The soul has a profound meaning to the self but a more profound meaning when it comes to leadership. A leader's soul is not only related to his or her sense of self; it is also a collective representation of an organization. The leader's soul has the ability to produce a compounding effect as it has the power to touch all individual souls associated with the organization. In other words, the leader's soul is the essence of the organization, the collective soul of the organization, the organization's center. When that essence, collective soul, or center becomes strong and positive, then the state of the organization also becomes strong and positive. If it weakens or becomes negative, then the entire organization suffers.

The essence of leadership is eternal and indestructible. It has the power to disseminate positive energy, hope, and vision. One vivid example of this is the leadership of Dr. King. His leadership in the civil rights movement became engraved in the socio-political future of the United States. The essence of his leadership created a compounding effect in the United States and abroad. "I have a dream that one day this nation will rise up and live out the true meaning of its creed," he proclaimed on the steps at the Lincoln Memorial in 1963. "We hold these truths to be self-evident: that all men are created equal." These words signify the eternal, indestructible essence or soul of Dr. King's leadership.

## Finding Purpose in Times of Adversity

History has given us great leaders who have risen in times of adversity. Winston Churchill rose as a prominent leader when he led the British from the verge of defeat during World War II. Franklin Roosevelt rose as a value-driven leader when he led the United States through the Great Depression. Gandhi rose as a luminous leader and the father of India when he led his country against the rule of the British Empire. Each historical figure shows us that great leaders rise to greater purposes at the time of greatest adversities and need.

In the Bhagavad Gita, Krishna encourages Arjuna to rise to the greater heights for a greater purpose. "A warrior like you should not tremble at a time of conflict," Krishna told Arjuna. "For a warrior, nothing is more dignified than a war against the evil. A warrior should be pleased when confronted with a war, for it comes as an open gate to heaven" (2:32–33).

The notion of "an open gate to heaven" provides an opportunity to leave a legacy. The greater the adversity and the greater the height for a leader to rise, the more likelihood a leader will leave a legacy. When Arjuna is confronted with the greatest adversity of a war against his own kinsmen, he must pursue a greater purpose for the fight. The Kauravas were an evil clan, and to fight the evil forces was important for Arjuna to protect his and his family virtues, as well as to safeguard future peace and tranquility in the kingdom. If a leader follows the righteous path with righteous virtues, his legacy remains the same, regardless of victory or defeat. "Death means the pleasure of heaven and victory means the pleasure of the Earth," says Krishna to Arjuna, "so, rise up and fight!" (2:37). Gandhi's legacy was unfettered after his assassination. Dr. King's legacy was unfettered after his assassination. Decades after their deaths, we still remember them for the transformations they brought to this world. They continue to live in the legacies they have left behind.

In times of adversity, anger and hatred are common reactions. What did most of the Americans feel right after the 9/11 attack? They were angry against the terrorists. What kind of reactions did we see from the American leaders? They were angry, too. In spite of anger and hatred, the resolution focused on national unity and homeland security. American patriotism rose to greater heights when people were faced with the horrible adversity of a terrorist attack. In the days that followed 9/11, there was an incredible demand for American flags. Retailers reported an upsurge in flag sales as high as 3,000 percent.[3]

Suggesting the need to be calm in times of adversity, Lord Krishna says, "Anger gives rise to delusion. Delusion corrupts the mind, and a corrupt mind destroys the power to reason properly. Defeat is imminent when the power of reasoning is lost" (2:63). When a leader is faced with adversity, he or she should divert anger toward finding a greater purpose—a purpose that strengthens the organization.

## Eliminating Bad Apples

Throughout the Bhagavad Gita, we see that Krishna repeatedly encourages Arjuna to wage war and kill his enemies. Why would a godly incarnation like Krishna encourage killing? If we look closely, the metaphorical meaning of killing is different from its apparent meaning of bloodshed and slaying. The deeper meaning of killing, especially from a leadership perspective, is to weed out malicious people and other unconstructive factors from an organization.

In his popular book *Good to Great,* author Jim Collins states:

> The executives who ignited the transformations from good to great did not first figure out where to drive the bus and then get people to take it there. No, they first got the right people on the bus (and the wrong people off the bus) and then figured out where to drive it.[4]

In the context of Arjuna's leadership role and the battle of Kurukshetra, the deeper meaning of killing is "to get the wrong people off the bus." Removing the wrong people from the organization encourages the right people. Positive energy comes from the right people, who, in turn, help to build a lasting organization.

The Kauravas had wanted to get rid of the Pandavas, so they could rule with complete authority. They had attempted to kill the Pandavas. They had forced the Pandavas to leave their kingdom for thirteen years. Because of their selfish desire to own the kingdom, the Kauravas created an environment of mistrust and fear. Because of their arrogance, negotiation was impossible. As a result, war was unavoidable, and the elimination of the evil Kauravas was a necessity for future peace and growth. The battle of Kurukshetra was an opportunity for the Pandavas to stand up to the bullying Kauravas.

## Focus on Actions, Not Rewards

"You have the right over your responsibilities, and the proper actions required of it, but you don't have the right to the rewards resulting out of it," says Krishna (2:47). "You should never engage in an action only for the desire of the rewards, and you should not desire inaction" (2:47).

Why does Krishna emphasize actions and responsibilities? How can one become motivated to carry out one's responsibilities if there is no emphasis on rewards? Many people are drawn toward leadership positions because of rewards like money and power associated with those positions. Most companies motivate their workers by enticing them with rewards based on results and objectives. Many corporations practice a result-oriented approach known as Management by Objectives (MBO) to reward their workers.

Although rewards may be enticing, focusing solely on rewards can distract people from focusing on the quality of actions that lead to the results. Sometimes the temptation of obtaining quick rewards based on quick results can also create the temptation of forfeiting quality and long-term benefits. As a consequence, the results produced do not last long, and the organization suffers in the long run.

Today, we have learned the importance of processes. We have also learned the importance of continuous improvement of processes. Quality has become important in every organization. Krishna's emphasis on actions reflects the importance of processes and quality. By focusing on actions, we ensure the effectiveness of every step taken toward attaining a certain goal. When we execute every step effectively, good results are inevitable; and when good results are inevitable, rewards are also inevitable.

To draw a parallel in today's world, one may think of a football team. The coaches and players know what to accomplish—to win the games. However, wins are not easy. They have to focus on every play and every yard—on offense and defense. They must focus on each and every action of their offensive plays before they get to the end zone. They also have to focus on every action of their defense. These football actions are analogous to "focusing on actions." If there is a focus on actions and if the actions are executed well, it becomes less difficult to win the games.

It is also important to understand that Krishna's message is not to lose focus on the results. If his support was not for a better future for the Pandavas, he would have never supported them in the first place. Of course, one must begin with the end results in mind, so actions are properly aligned with the desired results.

Krishna further stresses that one should work hard without getting attached to the rewards (2:50). By carrying out one's responsibilities, rewards are inevitable, whether one chooses to accept them or not. For an effective leader, the real meaning of rewards goes beyond fame, fortune, and power. True rewards mean fulfillment of a purpose—a purpose of doing the common good rather than pursuing personal achievements.

## Chapter 2: Krishna's Leadership Lessons

- Self-awareness enables leaders to identify their strengths and weaknesses and use their strengths to lead their organizations.

- Leaders should not delve too much into the past or the present. Instead, their main focus should be aimed toward the future and the strategies to attain an organization's goals.

- Leaders become immortal when their leadership touches people's hearts.

- Leaders should understand that change is the only permanent thing in this world and that they are responsible for bringing about positive changes and transformations.

- Leaders should be resilient in their actions and should not be weakened by pain and pleasure.

- The essence of leadership can be eternal and indestructible if leaders become the source of energy and vitality for the organization.

- Leaders should know that conflicts and adversities provide opportunities to find a greater purpose for their organizations.

- Malicious people and unconstructive factors must be ousted from an organization.

- Leaders should focus on the leadership actions and responsibilities, not on potential rewards associated with the position.

# 3

## *The Leadership Responsibilities*

# Being Proactive

Lord Krishna described *karma yoga* in chapter 3 of the Bhagavad Gita. In Sanskrit, *karma* means a person's actions that determine the successive phases of his or her existence, and *yoga* is training through mind and body. In the context of leadership, karma yoga signifies a leader's actions and responsibilities toward the organization.

"Avoiding actions and work does not give a person his freedom. Excellence cannot be attained by inaction or by giving up work," Krishna counsels when Arjuna asks him about the path to the supreme state. "It is wise to be proactive when it comes to fulfilling responsibilities" (3:4–5, 3:8).

Krishna's discourses stress the leader's responsibility to take initiatives. A leader holds the ignition key to the organizational engine that provides the organization with momentum and the ability to move toward the desired destination. Although a leader may have experience and wise advisers, a leader must be a self-starter when it comes to taking initiatives. A leader must be able to motivate him- or herself. A leader must be aware of initiatives that deserve the highest priority and be motivated to take action.

For leaders, proactive-ness means more than simply taking initiatives. It means that a leader must acknowledge that he or she has a responsibility to make things happen. Whether maintaining progress or inducing a small change or a big transformation, leaders bear the responsibility to take initiatives on behalf of the organization.

When a leader loses his ability to be a self-starter, he cannot take initiatives and he cannot lead. His organization suffers when no one ignites the organizational engine. When this happens, the organization fails to gain momentum and cannot move toward its destination.

So, what does Krishna mean by attaining freedom from actions and work (as described in 3:4)? "Freedom," in the framework of leadership, is purely the relief from carrying out leadership responsibilities. A leader who ascertains the completion of tasks required to attain certain goals gains relief from having the responsibilities completed successfully. In many organizations where leaders are rewarded based on performance and results, this kind of freedom could manifest in the form of perks and incentives.

"Excellence by taking actions," in 3:5, is another key attribute of effective leadership. If a leader refrains from taking action, nothing can be done, let alone attain excellence. Excellence comes by putting one's best into every action. An action, which is carried out by taking all things into consideration, leads to excellence in the end. Krishna further describes excellence in chapter 18.

## Sharing Opportunities and Responsibilities

"The righteous one who accepts and shares the rewards of his actions is freed from sins, while he who works for self-interests incurs sin," Krishna says to Arjuna (3:13). Here, Krishna stresses a leader's responsibility to work for others, not for personal benefits only. In business terms, one could relate this to the "maximization of shareholder value" or "customer satisfaction." In political terms, an equivalent could be "for the benefit of the common people." The significance here is that a leader should work for the common good and share the rewards with the organization.

Today, many leaders are engaged in philanthropy. They think beyond the benefits of their organizations. There are a handful of great philanthropists who have made differences in the lives of people who are not directly associated with them or their organizations. For example, Microsoft chairman Bill Gates invests billions of dollars through his Bill & Melinda Gates Foundation to promote global health, education, and many public welfare services. The pharmaceutical magnate Eli Lilly, who founded the Lilly Corporation in 1876, established the Lilly Endowment that invests billions of dollars in education and community development.

A quintessential leader and philanthropist worth mentioning in this context is Ewing Marion Kauffman who founded the Marion Laboratory and the Major League Baseball team the Kansas City Royals. One of Kauffman's core values was to share the rewards with those who worked for him and his organization. He consistently shared company profits with his employees by sharing stocks with them, enabling them to reap the rewards of hard work they put in for the Marion Laboratory. He even held parties in appreciation of his employees and other close stakeholders of the company. Kauffman died in 1993; however, his legacy and values are still promoted through the Ewing Marion Kauffman Foundation.

The concept of a leader working for others does not necessarily mean that the leader does all the work. Leaders should delegate responsibilities and tasks. He should promote an environment in which each stakeholder identifies, acknowledges, and shares equal responsibility for the overall work and actions. Gandhi, for example, did not take the historic Salt March all by himself. Dr. King did not fight for the civil rights by himself. These leaders did their part, and followers played their role in the overall responsibilities of the organization or movement.

Speaking further on karma yoga, Krishna adds, "Work for the common good without selfish interests; the rewards of selfless work will take you to the supreme state" (3:19). The "supreme state" can be defined in several ways. From a psychological perspective, it refers to the highest level of consciousness. It is the highest level of self-awareness that transcends the physical world and the physical senses. To define it philosophically or theologically, it is the state of absolute oneness or the state of absolute non-duality. Most traditions interpret this non-duality as God, the Supreme Being. In the Bhagavad Gita, a frequent term is *Brahman*, the Sanskrit word for non-duality, the Supreme Being, or the supreme consciousness. (There is more discussion on this topic in subsequent sections and chapters.)

In the context of leadership, the supreme state refers to a higher level of leadership consciousness or awareness. Sharing opportunities and responsibilities without selfish interests are acts that symbolize this higher level of leadership consciousness or awareness.

## Influencing Others

One of the principal purposes of leadership is to influence others. A leader should influence others in a constructive way, so he can lead his organization toward a desired vision and goals. The subjects of his influence may be internal and external stakeholders of his organization. A leader determined to transform his organization in positive ways must influence not only stakeholders who help induce change but also stakeholders who need to undergo such a change.

Influencing others also gives an important dimension to leadership—it creates followership. A leader has no meaning unless he has followers, whether they follow by enforcement or through inspirational leadership. Standing in front of a group does not make anyone a leader. Leadership is not possible if no one follows.

Followership does not always happen by enforcing authority. An autocratic rule does not necessarily mean there is true followership. A true followership happens when a leader inspires and gives a sense of direction to the organization. The Bhagavad Gita teaches us to become inspirational and compassionate leaders, not to become autocratic leaders.

"People follow the noble ones. People follow the standards created by them," says Krishna (3:21). Throughout the history of humankind, we have heard many accounts of divine leaders such as Jesus, Moses, Mohammad, and Krishna. We follow their teachings because they have proved their nobility to humankind. Their teachings and leadership have inspired people to look forward to a better future. Referring to his divine responsibilities, Krishna says, "If I do not engage myself in work and action, then other people will do the same" (3:21–24). What if Krishna had not given the discourses of the Bhagavad Gita? What if he had befriended the diabolical Kauravas instead of the virtuous Pandavas? What if Jesus had not given his divine teachings? What if Moses had not received the Ten Commandments from God?

In recent history, great leaders like Gandhi, Dr. King, the Dalai Lama, Mother Teresa, and Mandela have demonstrated their nobility to the world, thereby creating a "followership" that spans beyond their immediate spheres of influence. Their philosophy and ideologies are celebrated not only by their organizations or associations but by people throughout the entire world.

The noble leaders not only create their own followerships, but they inspire their followers to become leaders. Just as Lord Krishna understood and acknowledged the leadership role of Arjuna in the battle of Kurukshetra, noble leaders understand that everyone is part leader and part follower.

Under the leadership of the legendary CEO Jack Welch, General Electric demonstrated that noble leaders promote an organization to create not only a followership but new leaders as well. Many who once worked under Welch later became prominent leaders. Larry Bossidy (Allied-Signal, Honeywell), Harry Stonecipher (Boeing), Walter Williams (Rubbermaid), Michael Lockhart (Armstrong Holdings, Inc.) and Chuck Lillis (Media-One) are some of the many leaders that once worked for General Electric under Welch.

## Selfless Service

The three basic motives for leadership are the desire for power, achievement, and affiliation.[1] Today, we do not see leaders who work without pay or without personal motive. Tell any political leader that he or she would not be given power or affiliation. Tell any CEO that his perks and incentives would be frozen. Would they be ready to lead without pay, power, or affiliation?

When Lee Iacocca became the president of the Chrysler Corporation in 1978, he realized his company had serious problems. He tried to save the company by changing its management and processes. In spite of this, the problems at Chrysler surmounted. Iacocca had to obtain government loans for the company. He urged the workers to accept salary cuts and reduced his own pay to $1 per year.[2] By 1983, he had led the company through rough times, had paid off the government loans, and had helped the company rebound. And through this entire process, he demonstrated that personal desires were not always the underlying motivation to lead an organization.

What about the motives of great leaders like Gandhi, Dr. King, Churchill, or Mandela? Were these leaders motivated by power, achievement, or affiliation? These great leaders were motivated not by their own needs but for the needs of their people. They wanted power and achievement not for themselves but for their organizations or causes. For them, "we" and "us" held more meaning than "I" and "mine." They were able to break away from a self centered mindset.

"Selfish desires and animosity are devils," says Krishna to Arjuna (3:37). "Selfish desires, which are seated in senses, mind and intellect, obscure self-awareness. Control your senses and win over the devils" (3:38–41). "Devils," "self desires," and "animosity" could be associated with the mindset of the Kauravas. According to the ancient Vedic tradition, detaching from selfish desires and animosity is necessary to attain complete self-awareness. Krishna said the same in the Bhagavad Gita. Effective leadership is not at all possible if a leader is full of personal interests and hidden agendas.

In the context of contemporary leadership, selfless service suggests *servant leadership*—a widely accepted leadership approach that considers a leader as the steward of his organization. A servant leader is someone who *serves* his organization rather than someone who is served.

## Attaining Self-Awareness

Krishna draws a logical approach of reaching a higher state of self-awareness. "Senses are higher than the body; mind is higher than the senses; intellect is higher than the mind; and soul is higher that the intellect," notes Krishna

(3:42). We tend to rely on our senses, mind, and intellect for our self-awareness. However, ancient wisdom suggests that our self-awareness becomes limited if we rely too much on our senses, mind, and intellect. A higher level of awareness is seated in our soul. The ancient Vedic traditions prescribe the practice of meditation to find self-awareness at the soul's level. (The concept of meditation is discussed in chapter 6.) Krishna suggests that one becomes a supreme leader by reaching the awareness level of the soul. The journey to this state of awareness starts from the physical senses. By controlling the senses from harmful elements like selfish desires and destructive emotions and behaviors, the awareness level of the soul can be attained.

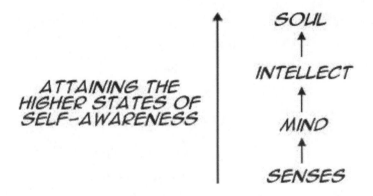

Let us quickly look at the definition of each state of this succession:

1.  *Senses*: Physical organs responsible for perceptions such as sight, smell, hearing, taste, and touch.

2.  *Mind*: The brain receives stimuli from sense organs and translates the stimuli into thoughts and feelings.

3.  *Intellect*: The capacity to reason from stimuli. The ability to rationalize things, objects, and events. The intellect is shaped by experience, training, and influence.

4.  *Soul*: The core of life—the spirit—that is embodied within the physical body, but not limited to the existence of the body or physical matters.

The succession of these states is especially important for an individual who wants to become an effective leader. A leader who focuses on the highest level of consciousness can look at the long-term organizational benefits that span above and beyond his own leadership role and tenure. A leader who has such a focus can achieve benefits that leave a lasting impact on the organization and its stakeholders.

Many people succumb to the needs of their senses due to circumstances or due to a lack of awareness. They look to the immediate benefits of their actions as perceived by their senses. Does it taste good? Does it look good? Does it sound good? People with a slightly higher level of self-awareness look to the mind and intellect. They question whether their actions are good or bad, whether the consequences would be good or bad. Based on their stimuli and their judgment, they create appropriate responses. However, their responses are limited to their own experience, training, and influence. In other words, they are limited to the outcomes of precedence. Their capacity to rationalize is limited to their own previous experience, the previous experience of their peers, teachers, or those who have influenced them in the past. Leaders with the highest level of consciousness look at the greater good, whether someone else has attainted that state before.

Great leaders like Gandhi and Dr. King led with the highest level of consciousness. They lived and led beyond the limitations of precedence and brought about sweeping transformations in the world. They were not limited to their senses, mind, and intellect. They were open to the world of possibilities through the highest state of self-awareness—the awareness of the soul.

At a deeper level, Vedic wisdom explains several levels of self-awareness or consciousness. These are covered in chapter 15.

## Chapter 3: Krishna's Leadership Lessons

- Excellence cannot be attained by inaction or by giving up work.

- Leaders have to be proactive and self-starters as they hold the ignition key to their organizations' growth and prosperity.

- Leaders should influence and inspire others in constructive ways, so they develop followership and inspire followers to become leaders.

- Selfish desires and animosity obscure self-awareness. They obscure the purpose of leadership.

- Leaders can become more effective if their self-awareness is at the soul's level.

# 4

## *The Leadership Intellect*

## Supreme Leaders

There are many things that influence our values and morality—our family, friends, and peers, to name a few. We are also influenced by the community in which we live or the church, temple, mosque, or shrine we attend. When it comes to leadership, we often look to those leaders whose values and morality align with our own values and morality. The reverence we hold for leaders and the conviction we have in their beliefs become strongest if leaders uphold common values and morality in times when they are at risk.

When racial segregation threatened the shared values and morality of African Americans, a great leader like Dr. King rose and fought for the people. When the British Empire restrained the shared values and morality of Indians, we saw a great leader like Gandhi rise up and fight for the people. Dr. King and Gandhi fought for the commonly shared values and morality of the people. Decades after their deaths, people continue to revere them and their values, mainly because they were able to uphold shared values and morality. Leaders around the world revere them and follow their paths because they set a benchmark for human values and morality.

Hundreds and thousands of years ago, Jesus, Mohammad, and Krishna left their marks on the earth as divine leaders. Not only did they preserve human values and morality, but they also set the highest standards for them. We still judge our values and morality based on the standards they created long ago. Their philosophies were adopted by humankind as superior belief systems.

The epic of the Mahabharata and the discourses of the Bhagavad Gita suggest that very few persons in Mahabharata knew about Krishna's divinity as a godly incarnation. He was mostly known as a charming, powerful individual. As he counseled Arjuna, Krishna reveals the divine purpose of his life to preserve human values and morality, saying, "When divine ideologies are forgotten, I shall manifest myself on the Earth. I am born time and again to defend the good and to destroy the evil and to reestablish the divine ideologies" (4:7–8).

Most of the time, we idealize divine leaders to be someone like Krishna, Jesus, or Mohammad. Their contributions to mankind are incomparable to other leaders in any circumstance, place, or time. We should also not forget that in every age, place, or circumstance, there are leaders who demonstrate the highest level of values and morality. They make extraordinary sacrifices for the sake of humanity.

In the recent history, Mother Teresa, Dr. King, Albert Schweitzer, Gandhi, and Henry Dunant were some of the many great leaders whose ideologies and belief systems were equally powerful in their own ways. Present-day leaders like Mandela, the Dalai Lama, and Desmond Tutu are other prominent leaders who have left lasting marks on the world.

## Supreme Leaders of Our Time

- **Mother Teresa:** She left her home (Macedonia) at eighteen to join the Sisters of Loreto who had a mission in India. After teaching at a convent school in Calcutta, India, she established the "Missionaries of Charity" whose main mission was to take care of the poor. By the 1990s, her charity had spread to more than forty countries with over one million workers helping people in poverty.

- **Dr. Martin Luther King Jr.:** In the 1950s, he was already a prominent figure in the civil rights movement of the United States. In 1957, he was elected president of the Southern Christian Leadership Conference that promoted the civil rights movement. He strongly advocated racial equality in spite of numerous arrests and assaults. He was assassinated in 1968. Dr. King is remembered for his vision for the civil rights movement and racial harmony.

- **Albert Schweitzer:** He was a pastor and a musician in France before beginning his medical studies. When he earned his medical degree in 1913, he founded a hospital in Lambaréné, Gabon. At Lambaréné, he worked as a doctor and surgeon, pastor and writer. Before his death in 1965, he made several contributions to the poor communities of Africa.

- **Henry Dunant:** In the earlier years of his life, he was a wealthy businessman. During a journey through an Italian town of Solferino, he witnessed a bloody battle, which inspired him to write *A Memory of Solferino* in 1862. One of the themes of his book was the proposal to form national relief societies to provide care for the wounded in battles. An international conference was called for, which soon became the Red Cross in 1864, with the signing of the Geneva Treaty. The Red Cross movement transformed into an international movement, serving the wounded in the battlefields and helping the needy in natural catastrophes.

- **Nelson Mandela:** For his resistance against South Africa's apartheid, he was sentenced to life imprisonment in 1964. In spite of twenty-seven years in prison, he continued to support the fight against apartheid and became the symbol of the antiapartheid movement. After his release in 1990, he became a key figure to abolish apartheid in South Africa. He served as the first democratically elected president of South Africa between 1994 and 1999.

- **The Fourteenth Dalai Lama:** Tenzin Gyatso was recognized by Tibetans as the fourteenth reincarnation of the Dalai Lama—an incarnation of peace and compassion. He served as the head of the state of Tibet until 1959 when he was forced into exile in India. Since then, the Dalai Lama has been a global ambassador of the Tibetan people, advocating Tibet's freedom and preaching the universal message of love and peace among all people and nations.

All of these leaders were awarded the Nobel Peace Prize for their contributions to humanity.[1]

# When to Act, When Not to Act

In chapter 4 of the Bhagavad Gita, Krishna speaks of the judgment of actions and inactions. He notes, "A wise person sees action amidst inaction and inaction amidst action. When he acts, his actions are done with complete self-awareness" (4:18).

When to act and when not to act has great importance to leaders as decision making is an integral part of leadership. We have heard stories about generals and commanders in wars who wait until the last minute to signal their troops to attack their enemies or many who attacked early to subdue an unprepared enemy. Many business leaders remain silent when the market is competitive and volatile, and many rush to create strategies to be the most competitive in the marketplace. Some leaders respond to situations reactively, and many leaders respond to situations with thorough and proactive planning and analysis.

"Actions amidst inaction" suggests being proactive, or thinking and acting in advance. The meaning of "inaction amidst action" is quite arcane. How can we not act when there is so much happening around us? Can a leader sit back and relax when his organization is moving in a certain direction? When the organization moves, a leader must steer the organization in the proper direction. In some cases, a leader's mere presence can inspire an organization to move forward and make progress.

Even if one is not actively involved in an event, that person can be mentally engaged in the activity. One can gather thoughts by observing activities. We hear people say—"I'll be there in spirit" or "My heart goes out to you." A person's association with an action or an activity is not always measured in terms of physical presence or bodily action. A person may have a higher level of awareness of an event even if he is not directly involved in it. The state of awareness or consciousness such as knowledge and essence are some examples of actionless states. The ancient Vedic tradition suggests that a simple act of paying focused attention provides more meaning than an act of active but useless physical involvement.

A leader's essence can hold greater meaning for an organization such as being a symbol of hope and inspiration. Sometimes leaders and their values serve as symbols to motivate an organization to attain its goals. Actionless states such as knowledge, essence, and vision transcend the leaders themselves.

One example of this is President Kennedy's vision. On May 25, 1961, Kennedy laid out his vision of landing a man on the moon and returning him safely to the earth. Kennedy was aware of the rising competition with other nations in the exploration of the space. He realized the necessity of making the United States the first nation to put a man on the moon. Although Kennedy was the one to present the vision of the moon mission, the United States did not land man on the moon until 1969 during President Richard Nixon's administration. Kennedy's vision, which was an actionless state, later became perpetual in terms of shared values and the future growth of the space program.

When there is an uncertainty as to whether to act, it is important to understand the benefits of the actions. Krishna says, "The goal of actions is to gain wisdom" (4:33). Is this really applicable in today's world? Gaining wisdom alone may not be a key motivator to act in today's world. In a growing laissez-faire world, leadership and perks usually go hand in hand. The goal of leadership actions should be to gain tangible or intangible benefits that have lasting impacts on the organization. Such benefits should maximize the shared values of the organization. Such benefits should maximize the potentiality of the people within the organization.

## Knowledge and Actions

Arjuna was confounded by Krishna's advice on action and inaction. "If both paths—path of action and path of inaction—lead to the supreme state of self-awareness or consciousness, then which one is better?" Arjuna questions Krishna (5:1). To this question, Krishna answers, "Both actions and inactions lead to the supreme state. However, the path of action is better than the path of inaction" (5:2).

Knowledge, which we identified earlier as an actionless state, is a necessity for purposeful action. An action without knowledge may become useless action. For leaders, knowledge is necessary because it gives them the ability to judge the causes and the consequences of their actions. Likewise, knowledge also gives them the ability to evaluate situations where an action may not be required at all.

The understanding of a collection of completed actions leads to an experience. Positive and negative experiences teach us what to do and what not to do in the future, when to act and when not to act. Hence, there is a strong correlation between knowledge and actions, which Krishna summarized by saying, "The wise see no difference between knowledge and actions" (5:4). An action leads to knowledge, and knowledge leads to actions. They complement each other.

This cyclical process of learning (knowledge) and acting (action), if used appropriately, accumulates proper knowledge and creates efficient actions. For an effective leader, a higher level of knowledge produces purposeful actions.

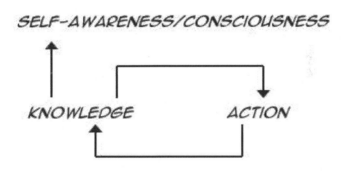

## Learning from a Mentor

Krishna and Arjuna were not only friends; they also had a mentor-mentee relationship. Krishna's discourses are teachings to his friend and mentee, Arjuna. Krishna emphasizes this mentor-mentee relationship when he says, "Learn from those who have realized the truth and question him with reverence and devotion" (4:34).

The significance of the mentor-mentee relationship between great leaders is evident in many historical accounts of leadership. In the Greek epic

*The Iliad,* Phoenix was a mentor to Achilles. In historical Rome, Pompey the Great was the mentor to Julius Caesar before they became enemies.

In the recent history, the twenty-sixth President of the United States, Theodore Roosevelt, mentored William Howard Taft, who later became the twenty-seventh President of the United States. The Russian President Boris Yeltsin mentored Vladimir Putin, who later became the Russian president. Dr. King mentored Jesse Jackson, who later became a prominent civil rights leader.

The National Football League (NFL) is also popular for creating many great mentor-mentee relationships. Some of the most popular NFL coaches like Mike Holmgren, Steve Mariucci, Mike Shanahan, Jeff Fisher, and Pete Carroll were mentored by celebrated NFL coach Bill Walsh. Other great coaches like Dan Reeves and Mike Ditka were mentored by Tom Landry, the famous coach of the Dallas Cowboys.

For effective leadership to flourish, a leader has to learn from a mentor who can teach values that surpass a particular leadership position. The lessons from the mentor-leader should hold values that are more meaningful in terms of leadership and organizational development. The key benefit of mentorship is that the mentee gains perspective from their mentor's experience and wisdom rather than blindly following the lessons or their interpretation of lessons. It is also necessary for the mentee-leader to find the right mentor, so he or she is not misled. Likewise, without the right mentee, a mentor's efforts might go wasted. The mentee must have the conviction and patience to learn from the mentor. It truly takes a great leader to create another great leader.

## Conviction of Learning

As Krishna presents his divine discourses, Arjuna listens to him patiently and with absolute faith. He questions Krishna with reverence and devotion, and Krishna answers his questions with equal respect. Krishna had a special lesson about the path of learning. He states, "The one who has faith and conviction, and has control over his senses gains the supreme knowledge" (4:40).

The path to supreme knowledge—the knowledge that helps attain the highest level of self-awareness—is not an easy one. For leaders, that path is more difficult as they have to lead their followers and organization through it. They have to use their intelligence and strength by learning from their experience and trainings. When they walk on that path, their mentors and advisers are only at their side, encouraging them or advising them but not leading them. Leadership can be lonely. When it comes to making decisions and taking bold initiatives, leaders are often on their own. The only companionship they have is their own faith and conviction. Moreover, faith and conviction are not possible if leaders have not achieved high levels of perseverance and tolerance.

All leadership situations cannot be tackled through counsel from mentors and advisers or by reading the great texts on leadership. For example, the challenges Gandhi faced as a leader were unique and had not been undertaken by other leaders before him. Nonviolent resistance, at a larger scale, was unheard of before Gandhi. So how did Gandhi formulate nonviolent resistance when no one had counseled him to use such a practice as a large political movement? Writers, politicians, and ancient texts had influenced Gandhi on the subject of *ahimsa*, the Sanskrit word for nonviolence. He was also influenced by people like Leo Tolstoy, who promoted nonviolence in his writings; the nonviolence teachings of Rajchandra Ravjibhai Mehta (Raychandbhai), whom he considered as a spiritual mentor; and the ancient texts like the Bhagavad Gita and the *Upanishads*.

While Gandhi had to forge his own way to lead the people of India through nonviolent means, these sources influenced Gandhi in many ways, nevertheless. The true materialization of the nonviolent resistance sprouted from Gandhi's introspection with his inner self, as evidenced from his philosophy of meditation. "Silence is a great help to a seeker after Truth like myself," said Gandhi. "In the attitude of silence, the soul finds the path in clear light, and what is elusive and deceptive, resolves itself into crystal clearness."[2] This type of philosophy is also evident from the life of Siddhartha Gautama when he attained enlightenment through meditation and transformed into the Buddha—the enlightened leader. Therefore, Krishna's message on the conviction of learning is deeply rooted in the practice of meditation, which is explored in chapter 6.

## Chapter 4: Krishna's Leadership Lessons

- An effective leader should know when to act and when not to act.

- Knowledge is necessary because it gives leaders the ability to judge causes and consequences of their actions.

- For an effective leadership to flourish, a leader has to learn from a mentor who can teach values that surpass the leadership position itself.

- In the absence of mentors and guides, leaders can find leadership meaning and direction through meditation.

# 5

## *Qualities of an Effective Leader*

# Leading with Compassion

On May 13, 1981, Pope John Paul II was riding in an open car in St. Peter's Square in the Vatican City when a bullet struck him on the abdomen. Fortunately, the bullet did not damage his vital organs. The Pope was hospitalized and recovered shortly thereafter.

The world soon learned about the gunman, a man named Mehmet Ali Ağca. Mehmet was a professional gunman, a professional killer. He had professional training in weaponry and terrorist tactics. In spite of an attempt on his life, the Pope met him in 1983 and forgave him for the assassination attempt. There were reports that the Pope had even kept in touch with his family and met his mother in 1987.

Jimmy Carter, the thirty-ninth President of the United States, is popular as a crusader of world peace and human rights. After his tenure in the White House, he has dedicated his life to spread the message of peace and human rights around the globe. Every year, Carter and his wife Rosalynn get involved in Habitat for Humanity to build houses for the needy. He is well-known for his hands-on carpentry skills and building houses.

After his presidential years, Carter became actively involved as a conflict mediator around the world. He has helped mediate conflicts in North Korea, Uganda, Ethiopia, and many other countries around the world. For his exceptional role in spreading peace and compassion at home and abroad, Carter was the recipient of the 2002 Noble Peace Prize.

The aftermath of the terrorist attack on September 11, 2001, not only brought the people of the United States together, but it also brought the best out of leadership. The business world saw the emergence of a compassionate leadership style. Many business leaders identified the need for compassion to deal with their employees, customers, and partners.

Morgan Stanley was one of the tenants in the World Trade Center. After the terrorist attack on 9/11, the management at Morgan Stanley decided to set the physical and emotional welfare of the employees as a priority, which also gave the company a sense of unity and purpose.[1]

TJX lost seven employees aboard a plane that hit the World Trade Center. Shortly after the tragic incident, CEO Edmond English confirmed the names of the victims to his staff and arranged for grief counselors. He chartered a plane and invited the victim's relatives to the company headquarters in Massachusetts. He personally greeted the families when they arrived. English allowed his employees to take time off to deal with the tragedy; however, most employees felt embraced and decided to work and not take any time off.[2]

Compassionate leaders are more likely to bring about lasting transformation to their organizations. They are more likely to leave legacies after their terms. More importantly, compassionate leaders are also likely to create a culture of harmony and collaboration within their organizations. Ewing Marion Kauffman was one such leader whose compassion transformed his organization, Marion Laboratories, Inc. People who worked for Kauffman knew him as a compassionate leader, who empowered them to work harder for the organization. Today, the compassionate culture he created lives on with the Ewing Marion Kauffman Foundation. The Kauffman Foundation has been involved in promoting entrepreneurship and education.[3]

Every leader cannot be as compassionate as Pope John Paul II. It takes a big heart to forgive someone who tries to assassinate you, but simple and humble acts of compassion can go a long way as well. At eighty-one, why is Jimmy Carter personally involved in Habitat for Humanity? He can probably motivate and lead other people to build houses for the needy. He can focus on raising funds instead. Yet, his humble act of personal involvement gives him a different perspective on the meaning of compassionate leadership.

In the business world, it is difficult for leaders to act with compassion as most decisions are influenced by economic forces. One could argue that corporate giving is an act of compassion; however, it is often associated with tax breaks and sometimes associated with social responsibility. In the context of business leadership, compassion means fairness to the people that the business comes into contact with—customers, employees, and other stakeholders.

In today's challenging world, leaders constantly face situations that require decisions that may not favor everyone they affect. National leaders must make decisions that determine war and peace. Business leaders must make decisions on downsizing and divesting. Sometimes, great coaches have to decide whether to let a player go when he performs poorly. However, if the leaders are known for their compassion, their followers must have a higher degree of acceptance toward the leadership decisions and actions.

Stressing the need for compassion, Krishna tells Arjuna, "The enlightened people treat everyone as their equals. They attain the supreme state of consciousness by setting their mind to fairness and equality" (5:18–21).

Compassion allows leaders to promote equality and fairness among followers. The power of compassion helps leaders to see people as human beings first and then as followers. Leaders who see people solely as followers often fail to succeed as good leaders. They become autocrats and dictators who, typically, are later scorned in the pages of history. Leaders become effective when they show compassion toward their people and followers.

## Emotional Intelligence

For leaders, emotional intelligence is important in times of adversity and prosperity. Leaders who keep themselves composed at all times create an environment of perseverance and confidence within their organizations. Celebrating too much in times of prosperity and despairing too much in times of adversity makes a leader prone to failure. Leaders must have enough self-control over their emotions so as not to hinder their own success and that of their organizations. Referring to a leader's ability to manage his emotions, Krishna tells Arjuna, "The wise are neither elated by pleasure nor saddened by pain. They remain in a constant state of inner joy that comes with the supreme state of consciousness" (5:20–21).

In their research, Daniel Goleman, Richard Boyatzis, and Annie McKee (authors of *Primal Leadership*) found a striking link between leaders' emotional maturity and their performance.[4] They claim that the leaders' emotions are contagious, and their emotions can create a positive culture or work environment. Their research shows that a high level of emotional intelligence creates climates in which information sharing, trust, healthy risk-taking, and learning flourish.

In his book *Emotional Intelligence: Why It Can Matter More than IQ,* Daniel Goleman describes emotional intelligence as qualities that help people succeed at work and relationships.[5] The discourses of the Bhagavad Gita attest to the concepts of emotional intelligence, and its association with leadership already existed thousands of years ago in the Indian subcontinent. Throughout the Bhagavad Gita, we find discourses on the leadership qualities with respect to emotional intelligences, such as self-awareness, self-management, social awareness, and relationship management. These qualities help leaders attain the supreme state of consciousness, thereby becoming more effective leaders and creating leadership legacies.

## Altruism

The qualities of emotional intelligence help leaders become cognizant of their own emotions and behaviors, as well as the ones present in their organizations. The collective emotions and behaviors are embedded in the organizational culture. Self-awareness, which Goleman describes as the key ingredient of emotional intelligence, helps leaders identify their strengths and weaknesses, so they can use the strengths for the benefit of their organizations. A leader aware of his charismatic skills may succeed at influencing others with charisma and may thrive in a democratic or laissez-faire society. A leader aware of his aggressive style may thrive in a more autocratic environment even though it may not be the best style with which to lead in an increasingly democratized world.

Authority, money, and position usually come with leadership, but they also produce unnecessary and selfish impulses. Effective leaders identify the unnecessary impulses and focus on matters important to their organizations. This type of self-awareness and altruism help leaders become more effective, as they play important roles in their organizations. "The wise ones overcome impulses like unnecessary desires, anger, and fear that come from the senses," says Krishna, suggesting that leaders should have higher levels of emotional awareness. "They conquer their senses, mind, and intellect through the power of meditation and unite with the supreme state of consciousness" (5:23–28).

All human beings are susceptible to anger and fear. However, these behaviors create conflicting forces in leadership when perseverance and courage are needed most of the time. Anger distorts the ability to make right judgments, and fear hinders one's ability to take courageous initiative. Control over anger and fear is of great importance to leadership. Leaders must learn to divert anger and fear into productive, positive energy. By being or becoming aware of anger, leaders must identify its causes and find corrective measures instead of reacting abruptly to it. They must identify fear and suppress it to become stronger and bolder, to find new opportunities in courageous ways. Fearful leaders weaken and enfeeble their organizations.

Krishna also highlights the importance of meditation in overcoming unnecessary impulses. Although meditation is a subject of deeper meaning, its implication to leadership is that it allows a leader to maintain his focus on the vision and goals of the organization, group, or movement. In the next chapter, we will further explore the subject of meditation and its implications to leadership.

## Chapter 5: Krishna's Leadership Lessons

- Compassionate leaders promote equality and fairness among followers.

- Emotional intelligence is important in times of adversity and prosperity.

- Leadership positions come with authority and power that make them prone to selfish desires, anger, and fear. Unnecessary impulses must be avoided and channeled in positive ways.

- Leaders must know that anger distorts the ability to make right judgments, and fear hinders the ability to undertake courageous initiatives.

# 6

## *The Leadership Focus*

## Action and Focus

The discourses in chapter 6 center on the concept of meditation. Meditation is usually discussed in the context of spirituality and the mind-body-soul connection. In general, when one thinks of the word "meditation," one probably thinks of someone sitting comfortably with his or her eyes closed without any physical movement. This is the popular way of practicing meditation. According to the ancient Vedic tradition, meditation is the state of being in peace with our inner selves and the world around us, regardless of our physical state, events, or surroundings. In the context of leadership, meditation is the ability to focus and stay on course of the vision and goals. It is the ability to focus on the leadership's purpose while carrying out required tasks and actions.

In the Bhagavad Gita, Krishna emphasizes being focused while carrying out selfless actions, "Those who are engaged in actions without expecting rewards attain the goals of meditation" (6:1).

Why is action important to attain the goals of meditation? Leadership focus is required when there is a momentum or a need for momentum in an organization. A static organization has no need for leadership. When leaders move their organizations forward or upward, they need to take appropriate action and remain focused on the overall vision and goals. This focus helps leaders ensure that the actions they undertake lead their organizations to the desired goals.

Throughout the Bhagavad Gita, Krishna has emphasized the importance of *karma*—the Sanskrit word for "actions." When a person focuses more on the outcome than the actions, he should not expect a superior outcome. When he focuses on each action and undertakes those actions to the best of his abilities, then a superior outcome is inevitable. Focused actions, therefore, are also likely to produce meaningful outcomes.

There is also a deeper meaning of meditation as it relates to leadership. Ancient Vedic practitioners believed that the power of pure consciousness, attainable through meditation, was more potent than any other power in the universe. This is analogous to scientific developments of the past century based on the understanding of quantum physics. Science is able to achieve its greatest feats when scientists are able to understand the universe at the quantum level. The quantum level of human existence, which the Vedic tradition referred as the pure, supreme consciousness, is the source of true potentiality. Changes and transformations, which are the most important aspects of leadership, become profound and meaningful if they arise from pure consciousness.

A branch of meditation practice called the transcendental meditation has become popular as a problem-solving and creativity tool. Some of the leading practitioners of this form of meditation recommend people simply think about a problem statement before meditating. Although they do not claim that the solution will be presented right after meditation, this basic underlying premise of mediation is commonly believed by many Vedic seers, psychologists, and physicists—that is, our deepest psyche or the inner consciousness has the potential to solve anything, worldly or unworldly.

## Befriending Willpower

Whether it is leading a nation or a corporation, leaders constantly face challenges that require them to maintain a focused course toward a vision and goals. To remain single-minded requires a strong determination or willpower. To execute an extraordinary vision and goals, ordinary willpower does not suffice. Great leadership calls for great willpower. It takes great willpower to lead a nation to its independence and toward democracy. It takes great willpower to bring a sweeping transformation in a society or a nation. It takes great willpower to lead a corporation to become a market leader. Willpower is not only required in leading large entities like nations or corporations; it is needed for raising a virtuous family or leading a dynamic community as well.

At the age of thirty-three, Sergeant First Class Paul Ray Smith left his home, his wife, and two children to go on an assignment in Operation Iraqi Freedom. On April 4, 2003, Smith was in charge of a hundred-soldier platoon while on a reconnaissance mission around the Baghdad International Airport. The same day, Smith's platoon received an assignment of building a holding area for prisoners of war near the airport. The platoon found a location and started building a cell. Soon afterward, they were under attack from hundreds of enemy soldiers. The enemy started firing rifles, rocket-propelled grenades, and mortars at the platoon, wounding several soldiers. Identifying a severe risk to his fellow soldiers, Sergeant Smith took command of a machine gun on top of an armored vehicle. He started shooting at the enemy while ordering his platoon to evacuate. After the skirmish, Sergeant Smith was fatally shot by enemy fire. However, he had successfully helped his platoon evacuate to safety.

Two years after his death, Sergeant Smith was honored posthumously with the rare and prestigious Medal of Honor, the highest award for battlefield courage.

It is difficult for everyone to have willpower as strong as Sergeant Smith's. Not every leadership situation asks leaders to sacrifice their own lives. However, great willpower is required for selfless service, which is one of the ultimate leadership challenges.

Speaking about the necessity of leaders to have willpower, Krishna tells Arjuna, "Willpower is the friend of those who have befriended it. Willpower is the enemy of those who have not found it" (6:5–6).

## Willpower through Focus

Willpower does not come by itself. People are not born with it. Some may have a natural tendency to have more than others. People who have endured considerable hardship in their lives may have higher willpower as their heart and mind tend to be strengthened by difficult experiences. Some may have a tendency to gain willpower through observation and training. Family members, friends, and advisers could be sources of will-power. Nonetheless, is willpower always gained from external factors?

The source of willpower is within us. We may depend on external factors to gain willpower, but it is for us to utilize external factors to strengthen our willpower. We may have the most compassionate family, friends, and advisers, yet we may not be attuned to gain strength and will-power from their association.

In the Bhagavad Gita, Krishna recommends that a path of meditation is the greatest source of willpower. "Willpower comes from the inner self, which can be attained through meditation" (6:10). Recent studies have proven that meditation can greatly benefit an individual's psychological and physiological states. Many studies have shown that patients who meditated while receiving medical treatment were able to recover from illness sooner than those who did not meditate. These studies suggest that meditation helps us keep our mind and body in healthy conditions. Meditation vitalizes our mind with positive energy when we require focus and concentration.

Willpower increases by focusing the mind and believing in the self. A battle is already half won when we have willpower. In the epic of Mahabharata, the Pandavas were equipped with mighty warriors and weapons. However, they required willpower, especially on part of their leaders like Arjuna, who were weakened by their own emotions. By overcoming emotions and strengthening their willpower, the battle of Kurukshetra was already half won. Followers are also motivated when they see leaders with strong willpower. Motivating the army of the Pandavas required their leader Arjuna to achieve focus and willpower.

"By focusing the mind, the eternal truth can be achieved" (6:21). Krishna further advises Arjuna, "Once the self is aligned with the eternal truth, he cannot be moved by pain or sorrow" (6:22). In the context of leadership, the "eternal truth" is the organization's vision and goals. When leaders and their organizations are single-minded in purpose, they are more likely to attain their vision and goals. There may be ups and downs along the way; but with a single-minded focus, obstacles cannot hinder leaders from reaching their destination.

## Balancing Act

Leadership cannot be effective unless there is a balance between a leader and his organization. An organization is as good as its leader. A feeble or immoral leader can only damage the organization that he or she leads. A leader who has low self-esteem and little confidence harms an organization. For an organization to thrive, its leader has to be self-aware of his strengths and use them for the benefit of his organization. Likewise, the leader's personal weaknesses must not hinder the growth of the organization.

Many organizations often project mental images that reflect the essence of their leaders. These mental images are created by associating leaders with their organizations: Gates with Microsoft, Welch with GE, Mandela with South Africa, Gandhi with India, and so on. It is important for leaders to be cognizant of this association and create a balance between self and the organization.

Krishna speaks to Arjuna about keeping such a balance when it comes to managing one's responsibilities of self and the organization. Krishna says, "Too much or too less of worldly indulgence spoils meditation" (6:16–18). In the context of leadership, prioritizing only certain tasks can become an indulgence, which can spoil the broader focus required to forward the organizational vision. Moderation and balance are required to stay focused. Today, many leaders operate in a 24/7 mode. They sacrifice their personal and family lives for the sake of their organizations. They do not sleep much; they skip lunch to attend meetings. On the other hand, there are some leaders who take advantage of their organizational authority and perks to enjoy their personal lives. Over time, this other imbalance spoils focus and eventually breaks down the overall performance of the leader and the organization.

Sometimes personal and business ethics play an important role in maintaining a balance between the self and the organization. A leader will ask, "Do I make decisions that will benefit me? Or, do I make decisions that will benefit my organization?" Sometimes, the impulses of the leadership rewards like authority, money, and position make it difficult for leaders to make the right decisions, especially in the business world. Many decisions are driven by economic factors; and sometimes, decisions are based solely on economic forces that do not benefit the overall well-being of the organization.

Although economic drivers dominate business decisions, some leaders find compassion and empathy as means to create a balance between the self and the organization. On December 11, 1995, a large fire destroyed the Malden Mills—a privately held fabric mill based in Massachusetts. Thousands of employees immediately feared being out of job as the factory was completely destroyed. Using millions of dollars of insurance payout and millions more in loans, owner Aaron Feuerstein decided to rebuild the factory while keeping all employees on the payroll. He did not lay off a single employee. He could have retired lavishly with the money he had received from the insurance payout. However, by making his employees a top priority, Feuerstein enforced a culture of perseverance and endurance in his organization. His compassion toward his organization and people renewed employee morale, and employee productivity doubled once the factory reopened. Malden Mills was forced into bankruptcy in 1995; however, it is now reemerging from bankruptcy. It has received major contracts from big businesses, and its future is looking bright.[1]

## Practice and Self-Control

Meditation is not an easy discipline. It is not something easy to turn into a habit. Only few practice it, and very few have mastered it. In the Bhagavad Gita, Arjuna is bewildered by the topic. He asks Krishna, "Stilling the mind is like taming the wind? How can you meditate and tame the mind that is like the wind?" (6:33–34). Krishna replies, "It is true that taming the mind is like taming the wind. However, the mind can be tamed with practice and self-control" (6:35).

This discourse provides an important lesson on achieving focus through practice and self-control. Practice is something one does repeatedly until one has achieved excellence, whatever the standard of excellence is for a person or a group. To achieve great feats, focus should be consistent, so the mind remains pointed toward the vision and goals at all times. Self-control is an important pillar for being focused. By controlling emotional impulses and channeling them in positive ways, one remains calm and strong in adverse conditions.

Effective leadership requires more intense and conscious focus while maintaining discipline and self-control. Imagine maintaining a focus on a particular vision for decades. That's exactly what Mandela did. For his involvement in the African National Congress (ANC)—South Africa's principal organization for the liberation movement—and its defiance campaign against the South African apartheid, Mandela was imprisoned for twenty-seven years. During most of his prison years, he was allowed only one visitor a year and to write and receive only one letter every six months. However, his focus on ridding apartheid became more intense during his prison years.

Once his daughter Zeni Dlamini visited Mandela in his prison to show him her newborn daughter. Mandela named his grandchild Zaziwe, meaning "hope" in his native language.[2] The naming of his grandchild—hope—was a symbol of his single-mindedness of purpose and the vision for a free South Africa. Sometimes, practicing small and humble acts in a consistent manner can keep us focused.

## Chapter 6: Krishna's Leadership Lessons

- Meditation helps leaders create a high degree of focus and potentiality when it comes to initiating changes and transformations.

- Actions with focus give momentum toward the vision and goals of an organization.

- A leader's ultimate friend is his or her own willpower that resides within the inner self.

- A leader has to achieve a balance between the self and the organization. An imbalance spoils the focus toward the vision and eventually breaks down the overall performance of the leader and the organization.

# 7

## *Know Thyself*

## Self-Actualization

Chapter 7 of the Bhagavad Gita discusses the concept of understanding the inner self. The understanding of the inner self means knowing who *I am*. This knowledge is not about one's profession, skills, religion, ethnicity, or other background information. Rather, it is about one's nature, character, personality, and virtues. Ancient texts like the Bhagavad Gita, *Vedas*, and the *Upanishads* suggest that there are two main paths to understanding one's inner self. The first path is the practice of self-assessment, a powerful tool for self-discovery and introspection on one's true inner nature. In ancient times, meditation was a form of self-assessment to understand the inner self. The second path is through our relationship with our surroundings—people, beings, and things. The Bhagavad Gita explores the second path in chapter 13.

In today's world, people use different ways to conduct self-assessments. One may have his or her own way of assessing the self; that is, if the person is open to acknowledging his or her strengths and weaknesses. Sometimes good friends and family members point out our strengths and weaknesses. In organizational and individual development and general psychology, there are self-assessment tools like 360-Degree Feedback and the Hogan Assessment. These tools help identify one's personality traits and find areas for improvement.

The process of self-assessment leads to the identification of strengths and weaknesses. By correcting weaknesses and refining the strengths, one can realize one's full potential in life. Sometimes this process of correction and refinement can be arduous; however, it presents opportunities to improve our character and virtues.

Self-criticism is an important part of this refinement process. By being critical of our weaknesses, we can correct them. If I know I am an angry person, how do I overcome my anger? If I know I am a bad listener, how do I become more attentive? If I know I am not team oriented, how do I become a team player? Self-criticism requires acknowledging our weaknesses and making an effort to correct them. We become self-actualized when we can acknowledge not only just our strengths but our weaknesses as well.

According to Krishna, not everyone makes an effort to become self-actualized. Krishna notes that, "One in thousands seeks self-actualization and only a few find it" (7:3). Focusing on the inner self is not an easy task. When it comes to knowing one's true self, day-to-day life is too distracting. Work, family, and other daily responsibilities keep us busy. Furthermore, most of us do not easily acknowledge our weaknesses, and correcting them is a big challenge. Refining our strengths also requires rigorous discipline.

Why is the understanding of the inner self important to leaders? According to the philosophy of the Bhagavad Gita, leaders cannot be effective unless they have an understanding of their inner selves. Effective leadership comes from leaders who first understand who they are. They know their strengths and weaknesses. They are aware of their personality traits and their true inner nature. They also know how to utilize their strengths and values to overcome personal and organizational challenges.

Self-actualized leaders create benchmarks for individual and organizational values and principles. They are usually the people to see when there is a question of ethics. Their teachings become the litmus tests for our ethical dilemmas.

## Leadership Character

Krishna speaks of three kinds of human character—"*Sattvic, rajasic,* and *tamasic* are three fundamental types of character" (7:12).

*Sattvic* is the character of harmony and purity. It is the character of the wise and righteous ones who are close to supreme consciousness (7:17). *Rajasic* is the character of growth and movement, and *tamasic* is the character of demons whose intellect is corrupt and who perform evil deeds (7:15).

What is the most appropriate character for leadership? Is there a preference of one over the others? The tamasic or demonic character is certainly not what followers would like to see in a leader. We prefer the sattvic character—harmonious, inspirational, and virtuous leaders. Gandhi, Dr. King, and Pope John Paul II all demonstrated sattvic character. We do not often find leaders whose leadership resonates with harmony and virtues like theirs.

Sattvic leadership is especially necessary when people's basic values and rights are at stake. These situations need not always be a fight for independence or civil rights. In chapter 6, we discussed the leadership of Aaron Feuerstein, owner of the fire-destroyed Malden Mills. His generosity toward his employees was a demonstration of sattvic leadership.

In certain situations, the rajasic character may work better for leaders as the trait of growth and movement can lead us through adversity and challenges and provide organizational development. However, according to the teachings of the Bhagavad Gita, the sattvic character is the most appropriate character we should expect in a leader. Unlike sattvic leaders, rajasic leaders are restricted by the interests of *I, me,* and *mine.* Therefore, rajasic leaders cannot perform selfless service. Selfless service is an important trait of sattvic leaders. By being able to look beyond the boundaries of *I, me,* and *mine,* sattvic leaders have the potential for transformational leadership—the type of leadership that causes radical but positive change in structure or processes. Leadership character is discussed in greater detail in chapter 14.

| Leadership Character | What it means? |
| --- | --- |
| 1. Sattvic | Sattvic leaders are harmonious and virtuous. They work hard for self-actualization. They promote integrity and honesty. They are willing to serve others without selfish interests and make personal sacrifices for their organizations. Leaders like Gandhi, Dr. King, Mother Teresa, and Pope John Paul II demonstrated sattvic leadership. |
| 2. Rajasic | Rajasic leaders are agents of growth and expansion. They hold high ambitions for themselves and for their organizations. They set aggressive goals. However, they are not self-actualized. They cannot think beyond their own interests or the interests of their organizations. |
| 3. Tamasic | Tamasic leaders are demonic and corrupt. They are driven by their own personal interests and prejudice. They are not compassionate, so they do not hesitate to put their people in pain to achieve selfish goals. They bring discomfort to their organizations. Autocrats and dictators are examples of tamasic leaders. |

# Union with the Supreme Consciousness

Krishna points out four types of people—the distressed, seekers of wealth and power, seekers of self-actualization, and seekers of absolute supreme consciousness (7:16). The distressed are those who have no motivation and are usually miserable. They need help of inspirational leadership. In an increasingly materialistic world, most people are seekers of wealth and power and driven by worldly impulses and aspirations.

Few seek self-actualization and the absolute supreme consciousness. These types of people rise above worldly impulses and aspirations and strive to know their inner selves. Some have already acquired enough wealth and power to pursue higher goals, such as self-actualization. Some have detached themselves from wealth and power and have dedicated their lives to knowing the supreme consciousness. Whatever the path may be, Krishna says, "The wise one knows the impermanence of life and seeks the absolute supreme consciousness" (7:29).

In the context of leadership, we may ask how great leadership can flourish without the quest for power, if not wealth and other worldly matters. Don't great leaders have power and wealth? Many prominent leaders are known by their power and wealth. Some leaders are perceived to have too much power and wealth.

To understand these questions, we must first examine the true definition of leadership. According to the Bhagavad Gita, leadership is about influencing and guiding *others* in a positive way, not about hoarding power and wealth for personal benefits. Furthermore, Krishna's lessons teach us that, without knowing one's true self, effective leadership cannot flourish. True leaders know their inner selves first before inspiring and guiding others. True leaders use their power and wealth for the benefit of others.

## Chapter 7: Krishna's Leadership Lessons

- First know your inner self and then lead others. Without the knowledge of the inner self, one cannot lead effectively.

- Leaders should seek self-actualization by identifying their strengths and weaknesses. They should correct their weaknesses and refine their strengths.

- Leaders should build a *sattvic* character, the character of harmony and purity that inspires and uplifts people.

# 8

## *Faith and Leadership*

# Faith—A Leadership Instrument

Let us begin this chapter by examining the meaning of *faith*. In the context of the Bhagavad Gita, there are two relevant definitions. The most common definition is a confident belief in the truth, value, or trustworthiness of a person, idea, or thing. The second definition is spirituality or the theological virtues defined as the belief and trust in a supreme being. Both definitions are essential for leadership. In this chapter, we examine why these definitions are essential for effective leadership.

In terms of trust and confidence, leaders can be a symbol of faith if they have a credible leadership background. They must demonstrate an alliance with their group's values and principles. Faith, as a belief in God or a supreme being, is an important aspect of leadership in many places or environments where certain religions or dogmas are prevalent. Religion is one of the key foundations of many nations and communities; their structures and operations are based on key elements of their religion. Many nations and communities elect leaders whose religion conforms to their dominant religion.

Some nations are ingenuous about their collective religion. Although some nations are secular, they usually have a dominant religion that serves as a guiding force for their overall values and principles. Historically, we find faith (a belief in God) as a vital factor in the establishment of many nations. The importance of faith can be found in many nations' founding documents. Their declarations of independence and constitutions provide proof of their conviction in faith as a basis of governance.

Many great leaders of the world were highly influenced by the teachings of their respective faiths and religions. The values and principles they led with were primarily based on their personal spiritual upbringing. Gandhi's values and principles were based on the teachings of Hinduism, predominantly the teachings of the Bhagavad Gita. Dr. King came from a family of pastors; his grandfather and father were both pastors. Dr. King received his

PhD in Systemic Theology and also worked as a pastor. His speeches and writings attest to the fact that his deeply rooted values came from his faith.

Jimmy Carter, the thirty-ninth President of the United States and Nobel Peace Prize winner, is another noteworthy leader who is well-known for his dedication to faith and religion. He regularly spends time reading the scriptures and sharing his personal faith with friends and communities. He has written several books on faith, such as *Living Faith* and *Sources of Strength.* In his book *Living Faith,* Carter states, "It is only through faith that I can maintain a relationship with the omnipotent Creator and my personal savior. Without this, I would feel destitute."[1]

Leadership based on spirituality has also made profound impacts on the world. For example, as an exiled leader of Tibet, the Dalai Lama continues to fight for the liberation of his homeland while spreading the message of peace and compassion —essentials of Buddhist philosophy. His teachings have gained wide acceptance and a followership around the world. Pope John Paul II, another spiritual leader, created a worldwide followership by spreading the message of peace and compassion. Time and again, we see spiritual leadership eliminate political and economical boundaries—in some cases even religious boundaries—and successfully reach out to millions around the world.

In the business world, the most meaningful equation of faith is trust and confidence. Most businesses create a secular workplace where religion is not a core part of business values. In the United States, the legal framework requires every business to view religion as a non-detrimental factor for conducting business. Title VII of the Civil Rights Act of 1964 prohibits employment discrimination based on religion. Paradoxically, by promoting secular beliefs in the workplace, companies encourage basic values of faith and religion in subtle ways. Values such as compassion, selfless service, and personal development—fundamentals for business and religion—are promoted in many organizations. Studies have also shown that spiritually minded programs in the workplace deliver improved productivity.[2]

In a *Business Week* article from 1999, Michelle Conlin submits her findings: "A spiritual revival is sweeping across corporate America as executives of all stripes are mixing mysticism into their management, importing into office corridors the lessons usually doled out in churches, temples and mosques. Gone is the old taboo against talking about God at work."[3]

## US Presidents and Faith

The US presidency has always shown a strong alliance with faith in God. Here are some quotes from different US presidents.

*"God who gave us life gave us liberty."*[4]
—Thomas Jefferson, third President of the United States

*"The strength of our country is the strength of its religious convictions. The foundations of our society and our government rest so much on the teachings of the Bible that it would be difficult to support them if faith in these teachings would cease to be practically universal in our country."*[5]
—Calvin Coolidge, thirtieth President of the United States

*"Menaced by collectivist trends, we must seek revival of our strength in the spiritual foundations which are the bedrock of our republic. Democracy is the outgrowth of the religious conviction of the sacredness of every human life...."*[6]
—Herbert Hoover, thirty-first President of the United States

*"The spirit of man is more important than mere physical strength and the spiritual fiber of a nation than its wealth."*[7]
—Dwight Eisenhower, thirty-fourth President of the United States

*"Without God there could be no American form of government, nor an American way of life. Recognition of the Supreme Being is the first—the most basic—expression of Americanism. Thus,*

the founding fathers of America saw it, and thus with God's help, it will continue to be."[8]
—Gerald Ford, thirty-eighth President of the United States

"My faith is an integral part of my whole being, that's what faith is. I don't think you can separate your faith from who you are."[9]
—George W. Bush, forty-third President of the United States

# Who Do Great Leaders Look Up To?

When we talk about leadership, most of us look up to great leaders. In the business world, we look up to leaders like Jack Welch of GE, Andrew Grove of Intel, and Herb Kelleher of Southwest Airlines. In the political world, we look up to leaders like Churchill, Gandhi, Dr. King, and Mandela. In the spiritual world, we look to leaders like Pope John Paul II, the Dalai Lama, or Desmond Tutu. But to whom do these great leaders look for great and effective leadership? To whom did Gandhi look? Whom did Pope John Paul II admire? And Dr. King and the Dalai Lama?

Krishna says in his discourses that the *Brahman*, the supreme consciousness, is the supreme leader to whom we should all look. The theological meaning of Brahman is God. The metaphysical meaning of Brahman is the supreme consciousness. Krishna says, "Brahman is resident in every individual…. One who focuses on Brahman as the eternal, the transcendental and the inconceivable achieves the ultimate goal of life" (8:3, 8:9). By looking inward to the self, one can unite with the supreme consciousness and find the supreme leader, the God, that is present in every being. God, whose presence is at the highest level of consciousness, is the highest order of leadership and the ultimate source of our guiding values and principles. Leaders who bring about transformations and set the benchmark for leadership look up to the transcendental force of Brahman, the supreme consciousness.

In the business world, most of us may not easily relate the concepts of God, Brahman, or the supreme consciousness to business values and ethics. Nevertheless, if we look carefully, some fundamental business values are no different from the values taught by any faith or religion. Values such as empathy, confidence, awareness, and service are shared by religion and business. The concepts of emotional intelligence and spiritual intelligence are becoming popular in the workplace, especially among executives and managers. Both kinds of intelligence have a strong basis on the higher level of consciousness, and they can also be related to the fundamental values of operating a business or following a religion.

Unlike political leaders, business leaders do not usually discuss matters of faith and religion with other people. Most keep faith and religion as a part of their private lives. Yet, some business leaders talk about it openly, and some even practice it openly. S. Truett Cathy, CEO of Chick-fil-A, hosts a prayer service Monday mornings. Jeffrey B. Swartz, CEO of shoemaker Timberland, relies on his religious beliefs to make important business decisions and often consults with his rabbi on business problems. Swartz allows his employees forty hours off each year to volunteer at a charity of their choice. Krishan Kalra, CEO of BioGenex, often references the Bhagavad Gita for solving business problems.[10]

Michelle Conlin writes, "Once words like virtue, spirit and ethics got through the corporate door, God wasn't far behind." [11] In the near future, it would not be surprising to see the business world talk openly about spirituality, that is, in a secular way.

## Faith—The Greatest Emancipator

Many leadership situations arise when there is a need to liberate people and organizations from one setting or mindset to another. Whether it is about winning a war to find peace, capturing the market share to expand a company's worth, or transforming a society, leaders are responsible for finding ways to initiate change and transformation from one setting to another, or from one mindset to another.

We usually look for external objects to find our liberation. We say that only if we did not have this confinement or that confinement, we would be liberated. We say that we would be liberated if we had more freedom, more authority, and more power. We say that we would be liberated if we had more money and more qualifications.

According to Krishna, the true liberation is not attainable by looking to externalities or external objects: "The unification with Brahman—the supreme consciousness—is the ultimate liberation for an individual" (8:26). The true liberation is attainable by first looking into the inner self. The ultimate liberation needs to come from within.

This knowledge is especially important for leaders who seek liberation for their people and organizations. Why did no one before Gandhi boldly think of liberating India? Why did no one before Dr. King boldly think of liberating African Americans from civil restraints? Why did no one before Mandela boldly think of liberating South Africa from its apartheid? Leaders like them were able to look into their inner selves first and find liberation before they were able to lead and inspire others to find their liberation. By looking into their inner selves and exploring their inner consciousness, these leaders were able to realize their full potential. By finding their own potential, they were able to lead and inspire other people. They were able to help people explore their inner selves and realize their potential.

## Chapter 8: Krishna's Leadership Lessons

- Leaders should know that faith, whether one considers it as trust and confidence in the inner self or spirituality, is the ultimate instrument of leadership.

- Leaders should look to God as the ultimate and transcendental leader.

- Before liberating others, leaders should look into their inner selves first and find liberation in their own inner consciousness.

# 9

## *Realizing the Ultimate Potential*

# Universality of Supreme Consciousness

Krishna tells Arjuna that "The *Brahman*—the supreme consciousness—is transcendental and permeates the universe" (9:4). The core nature of the inner consciousness, which is filled with compassion and selfless service, is universal to all traditions and faiths. When it comes to effective leadership, compassion and selfless service are key traits leaders must have. When leaders lack compassion and selfless service, they eventually lose respect and become scorned by the world or their followers. They become tyrants and dictators. However, if leaders are compassionate and willing to provide selfless service to people, they are likely to leave a legacy that stays with the people even after their tenure ends.

Gandhi and Dr. King were two of the few leaders in the world who led with compassion and selfless service. They sacrificed their lives for the service of their people. New leaders are born time and again. Yet, the leadership effectiveness of Gandhi and Dr. King surpasses most of the modern-day leadership scenarios. They created a benchmark for leadership.

The business world also thrives when it operates with compassion and selfless service. In today's world, businesses are evaluated on how well they treat their people—customers and workers. Businesses are rewarded and punished by the degree of customer satisfaction. If they lose respect and loyalty from their customers, they can no longer operate profitably, let alone compete in the marketplace.

Organizations thrive when they treat their employees well. Respecting employees translates into higher productivity and lower turnover. Many organizations acknowledge the importance of personal and professional development at work. They implement formal and informal programs to develop employees—not only to make them better workers but to make them better human beings as well.

The advent of the information age has also required organizations to change the ways they treat their employees. Organizations can no longer treat employees as they did during the industrial age when direct control over employees resulted in more productivity. The information age requires organizations to *empower* employees to make them more productive. This means organizations, especially leaders, need to understand that today's employees need inspiration and motivation to perform work. Inspiration or motivation is not necessarily about paychecks and perks, however. Today, employees need to be inspired and motivated at the levels of the heart and the spirit. They must be given a sense of purpose and goals in order to perform at optimal levels.

During the peak of the Internet bubble of the late 1990s, many privately held technology companies rushed to go public. In spite of the opportunity to earn billions of dollars, CEO of SAS Institute Jim Goodnight turned down the prospect of going public. Goodnight surveyed his employees, and a vast majority of them voted against going public. He could have simply listened to the advice of investors and had taken SAS public if he had wanted. However, he made the conscious decision to listen to his employees. By doing so, Goodnight saved his company's enduring culture. SAS has repeatedly been featured as a benchmark company in many newspapers, journals, and television programs. Contrary to other public companies that did not survive the Internet bubble, SAS has continued to grow with an incremental hiring rate and a decreasing turnover rate.

Goodnight may or may not have operated with an awareness of supreme consciousness. However, the fundamental idea is the same. The decisions he made for SAS show that he acted with compassion and selfless service. When leaders acknowledge the universality of the supreme consciousness—consciously or unconsciously—they can promote enduring positive values in their organizations. Organizations with compassion and selfless service can attain full potential in their day-to-day operations and in their vision and goals. They create a win-win environment where everyone can work and live happily.

## Power of Positive Intensions

Leadership requires steering an organization to reach to a desired destination. Vision and goals, derived from leadership thoughts and intentions, are required to arrive there. Generally, the cause and effect of the perceived reality and the desired intentions create the vision and goals one wishes to attain.

What is the perceived reality for leaders? Apart from their position, authority, and the organizational state, leaders are constantly affected by the political, social, and financial realities. They are affected by the common values and principles of their groups. The culture and norms of their organizations are other realities they have to face.

In the Bhagavad Gita, Lord Krishna repeatedly emphasizes that one should cultivate positive thinking full of compassion and selfless service. Likewise, leaders have to cultivate positive thinking in their thoughts and intentions. If there is a conflict, leaders should cultivate the thought and intention of attaining peace. If there is a famine, they should cultivate the thought and intention to provide food for their people. If there is poverty, leaders should cultivate the thought and intention of achieving prosperity.

Cultivating positive thoughts and intentions is important for attaining supreme consciousness. One should remember that the supreme consciousness is devoid of negativity. In chapter 6, Krishna stresses the necessity of consistent focus to get to this highest level of consciousness. This focus is also necessary to sustain positive thoughts and intentions. Only when positive thoughts and intentions are sustained can leaders attain and lead with the supreme consciousness.

Krishna says, "Those who focus on the supreme consciousness are never forsaken from their welfare" (9:22). Once an individual focuses on the inner consciousness, that person realizes the full potential in life. When a person is confident on seizing the full potential of the self, he can bring about sweeping transformation. He can bring about revolution like no other in history. By realizing the full potential of the inner consciousness, that person transcends the wants and needs of the physical world. Fulfillment of physical wants and needs becomes abundant but insignificant in the context of the higher goals in life.

## Finding the Ultimate Goal

For most of us who are busy with our everyday lives, the notion of the supreme consciousness seems too far-reaching. External distractions usually divert our attention away from our inner self. Does this mean that the supreme consciousness is beyond our reach? Is the supreme consciousness beyond the reach of everyday people and followers? Is it true that only saints can find supreme consciousness? Must one be a pope or the Dalai Lama to find it?

One of the main messages of the Bhagavad Gita is to find the supreme consciousness without giving up one's everyday life and everyday responsibilities. One does not need to be a saint or another major religious figure to find supreme consciousness. Anyone can achieve it; everyone has access to it because the supreme consciousness resides in the inner self of every being.

Krishna says, "Even if one is at fault, if he or she focuses on the supreme consciousness, that person quickly becomes righteous and finds lasting contentment" (9:30–31). This discourse explains that everyone can find greater purpose in life by focusing on inner consciousness. This means that the Pope, the Dalai Lama, and the great saints are not the only ones who can achieve supreme consciousness. Normal human beings are not the only ones who can reach their inner selves. Even criminals and persons who have committed wicked acts in the past can find it—that is, if they choose to seek it.

In the context of organizational behavior, the awareness that everyone can develop to their full potential is a very important concept for leadership and management. By harnessing the power of the inner self, organizations can achieve maximum productivity. The power of the inner consciousness can develop good citizens and good workers. More importantly, the focus on the inner consciousness is important for developing leaders. With this power, a non-leader can develop into a leader, or a bad leader can turn into a good leader. More and more companies today find that leadership development is an important part of an organization. These companies acknowledge that leaders can be developed by training and through discipline.

## Chapter 9: Krishna's Leadership Lessons

- When leaders acknowledge the universality of the supreme consciousness, they promote enduring values like compassion and selfless service in their organizations.

- By cultivating positive thoughts and intentions, a leader can attain supreme consciousness, which, in turn, helps the leader attain his full potential for self and the organization.

- The welfare of the self and the organization is attained by focusing on the supreme consciousness.

# 10

## *The Inner Power*

## Seat of All Virtues

"The supreme consciousness is the source of all qualities—qualities such as knowledge, wisdom, temperance, forgiveness, truthfulness, self-control, nonviolence, prudence, contentment, dedication, charity, and recognition" (10:4–5). The ultimate bearer of these qualities is the inner self. These qualities are seated in the inner consciousness. To master these qualities, we generally look outward; and with observation, experience, and practice, we enhance these qualities in the self.

If we reflect on the lives of supreme leaders like Gandhi and Dr. King, we see that they both incorporated most of these qualities into their lives. In fact, they set the benchmark for these qualities. If they were ordinary human beings before they were supreme leaders, where did they acquire such qualities? Who taught them to surpass the leadership challenges that lay before them?

Both leaders derived their leadership qualities from their inner selves. By looking to their inner selves, they taught themselves these qualities of leadership. Gandhi was a very spiritual person, who was highly influenced by the Bhagavad Gita. He derived most of his leadership philosophies from the Gita. Dr. King's philosophies of life and leadership were also deeply rooted in spirituality and the Bible.

Dr. King was also influenced by the Gandhian philosophy. In his autobiography, Dr. King notes, "Gandhi was probably the first person in history to lift the love ethic of Jesus above mere interaction between individuals to a powerful and effective social force on a large scale…. It was this Gandhian emphasis on love and nonviolence that I discovered the method for social reform that I had been seeking."[1]

In chapter 10, Krishna further states, "The compassion of the supreme consciousness destroys the darkness of ignorance" (10:11). Compassion enables the mind to be open to others and their ideas. Especially in the context of leadership, compassion enables leaders to accept a followership with an open heart. Compassionate leaders are more willing to listen to followers, and they are more likely to act in the interests of their followers.

Compassion allows leaders to be fair to everyone in an organization. When leaders are fair to everyone, they promote among people an awareness that allows one to be cognizant of the self and surroundings. This awareness also empowers individuals in the organization. Awareness, therefore, eventually leads to knowledge and wisdom.

Compassion also allows intelligence to reside at all levels of the organization because compassion allows leaders to acknowledge everyone's potentiality in the organization. When intelligence is spread throughout the organization, it leads to a learning organization. According to Peter Senge, learning organizations are those where people continually expand their capacity to create results they truly desire, where new and expansive patterns of thinking are nurtured, where collective aspiration is set free, and where people are continually learning to see the whole together.[2] A learning organization, therefore, eradicates the dangers of ignorance and fosters the idea of empowerment of every individual in the organization. A learning organization becomes possible only when leaders lead with compassion.

## Power and Glory

Arjuna asks Krishna about the glories of supreme consciousness, "Krishna, explain to me the glories of the supreme consciousness that is universal" (10:18). Hearing this, Krishna describes the manifestation of the supreme consciousness that permeates throughout the worldly and non-worldly matters: "The manifestation of the supreme consciousness has no limit. All things that have power and glory are the manifestation of the supreme consciousness" (10:40–41).

How can the supreme consciousness bring power and glory? In chapter 9, we learned about the core nature of the supreme consciousness being filled with compassion and selfless service. The supreme consciousness is also the seat of all virtues as discussed in this chapter. If we look at the lives of Gandhi, Dr. King, and Pope John Paul II, we find that these leaders gained power and glory through compassion, through selfless service, and, especially, by having a virtuous character. Power and glory meant nothing to their authority and control; power and glory meant inspiring others and fighting for the common beliefs, values, and principles.

Many leaders try to achieve power and glory without compassion and selfless service and through authority, control, and selfish needs. They may succeed in achieving power, but their power is not long-lasting. Instead of glory, they get disrespect from their followers and their organizations.

In the political world, Hitler, Pol Pot, Saddam Hussein, and Slobodan Milosevic were some leaders who tried to gain power and glory through authority and control but failed to give lasting leadership for their respective nations and organizations. Some of them exercised cruelty and violence, which eventually led to their own destruction.

In the business world, some leaders fail to lead with compassion and selfless service, primarily because the business world is mostly driven by economic factors. Becoming profitable, gaining larger market share, and expanding shareholder wealth make the business world very competitive and less forgiving. Many business leaders are also blinded by power and riches that come with leadership positions. They fail to understand that compassion and selfless service are possible amid power and riches.

Among many business leaders who failed to lead by compassion, Albert Dunlap is one of the most infamous. Instead of compassion, his leadership philosophy was "mean business," also the title of the book he authored. Dunlap was best known for his ability to make extreme cuts—both in financial and personnel. He reached the epitome of his ruthless leadership career when he led the Sunbeam Corporation. Like most of the companies he had led, he terminated more than 50 percent of the Sunbeam workforce. Dunlap's downfall started when the accounting practices at Sunbeam were questioned, and the shareholders sued the company and Dunlap for misleading financial statements. Despite the lawsuits, Dunlap continued to lay off employees and cut costs. Eventually, the board of directors was forced to terminate Dunlap. By the time Dunlap's leadership career was over, he had already become well-known as "Chainsaw Al," "Rambo in Pinstripes," and "the Shredder."[3]

Although the business world is largely influenced by economic drivers, some business leaders acknowledge that money and finances are not the only aspects of doing business well. They recognize that social responsibilities are equally important, and they make customer satisfaction the mantra of their organizations. Social responsibilities and customer satisfaction are impossible without compassion and selfless service. Operating businesses with compassion and selfless service has proven that business expansion is indeed possible through non-economic forces.

The leadership challenges of Aaron Feuerstein, CEO of Malden Mills, defied the generally accepted economic models of doing business, as he led with compassion and selfless service. By doing so, Feuerstein created a lasting leadership legacy and helped sustain his organization in the long run.

## Chapter 10: Krishna's Leadership Lessons

- Good virtues reside in the inner self—the seat of the supreme consciousness. Leaders should look into their inner selves to bring out the best of their virtues.

- Compassion, on leaders' part, leads to fair treatment of everyone in the organization. Compassion leads to self-awareness, open communication, and open collaboration. Most importantly, compassion creates a learning organization.

- Leaders achieve lasting power and glory by exercising compassion and selfless service.

# 11

## *Seeing the Big Picture*

# The Ultimate Vision

Arjuna is convinced that the power and glory of the *Brahman*—the supreme consciousness—are the ultimate rewards for an individual and, especially, for a leader. He slowly deciphers the true essence of Krishna and his teachings, and he is now convinced that Krishna is an enlightened leader, someone who speaks with the awareness of the supreme consciousness. Realizing the true potential of his friend and his charioteer, Arjuna requests of the leader, "Oh Krishna, if you think I am a deserving person, I wish to know your true essence" (11:3–4).

Upon hearing his friend's plea, Krishna responds, "The ultimate vision of my divine essence—the embodiment of the supreme consciousness—is not possible without the divine eyes" (11:8). Then Krishna grants Arjuna the divine vision, so he can see what his five senses cannot perceive. As soon as Arjuna receives this vision of grandeur, he beholds an unconquerable sight. The *Virat Rupa*, the supreme form of Krishna, stands before him. (In Sanskrit, *Virat* means "supreme," and *Rupa* means "form.")

Arjuna is captivated by the majestic sight, as he witnesses the powerful rays of the Virat Rupa penetrate the universe: "Your splendor is brighter than the brilliance of thousands of suns" (11:12). The supreme form embodies all material and nonmaterial forms. Arjuna sees all types of gods unified with the Virat Rupa. Great sages and saints emerge from the supreme form. All kinds of beings also emerge from the Virat Rupa. The sight is very difficult to grasp, even with divine vision. Arjuna cannot figure out the beginning or the end of the supreme form. He says to Krishna, "The entire universe is pervaded by the supreme form in all directions" (11:20).

Arjuna acknowledges that the sight of the Virat Rupa is overpowering: "I am overwhelmed and frightened by your supreme form" (11:24). He also sees the vision of his enemies, the Kauravas, being annihilated by the power of the supreme form (11:26–29). "Oh great one, the vision of your supreme form mystifies me," says Arjuna. "Please tell me who you are"

(11:31). Arjuna kneels and bows his head at the Virat Rupa. In response, the Virat Rupa says, "I am time—the destroyer of all, including the enemies that stand against you in this battlefield. Therefore, arise for battle. Conquer your enemies and win your sovereignty" (11:32–33).

After presenting the supreme form, Krishna takes back the divine vision from Arjuna. Now in his original human form, Krishna reiterates, "Arjuna, through dedication and focus, those who make the supreme consciousness as the ultimate goal in life will eventually unite with it" (11:54–55).

The presentation of the Virat Rupa, the supreme form, may sound mystical to a modern-day reader; however, there is a deeper meaning of the Virat Rupa in the context of leadership.

## Systems Thinking

In a philosophical or theological perspective, the Virat Rupa has been described as the ultimate, supreme form of God. As described in the Bhagavad Gita, the Virat Rupa is the source of all living and nonliving matter. In the leadership context, the metaphorical meaning of the Virat Rupa is deeper, which deserves a closer examination. The supreme form symbolizes an examination of "the big picture," or the approach of systems thinking from the standpoint of contemporary management science. During the discourses in the Bhagavad Gita, Krishna reveals the big picture of supreme consciousness, the Virat Rupa, to his friend Arjuna. By revealing this, Krishna suggests that, in every leadership situation, it is important for leaders to look at the overall strategic picture, the core to systems thinking.

The concept of systems thinking has evolved through many years of study by many scholars, most notably by Peter Senge, who is considered one of the top management gurus. In his influential book *The Fifth Discipline,* Senge says we can understand a system by contemplating the whole, not any individual part of the pattern.[1] He adds, "Systems thinking is a discipline for seeing wholes. It is a framework for seeing relationships rather than things, for seeing patterns of change rather than static snap-shots."[2] The analogy of systems thinking, in the context of the Bhagavad Gita, is the Virat Rupa. Both systems thinking and the Virat Rupa suggest an approach of looking at the overall picture.

The approach of systems thinking is also a discipline of looking at the interrelationships of an object or a thing. Systems thinking is necessary in most cases because complexities overwhelm us.[3] If we look around in our daily lives, we see many complexities. When we drive, for example, we see the complexities of traffic. Especially when we get stuck in a traffic jam, we are stuck in a web of interrelated complexities. If a wreck blocks the road ahead of us, then someone could have been driving recklessly or talking on the phone before hitting another vehicle. The person talking on the phone could have been in a stressful situation in his life. The event leads to the wreck, which has a cascading effect of other events that may not be directly related to traffic.

Another example of complexity is the existence of a human being and his or her relationships with other human beings and the physical sur-roundings. The individual identity is not derived solely from the individ-ual self. One's skills, qualifications, and accomplishments count toward that identity. However, without the recognition of those skills and accom-plishments by other individuals or institutions, the individual identity has no meaning or value. Similarly, the physical or biological makeup of an individual is also linked to parents and their family trees. A person's height, color, and other genetic attributes are connected to an ancestral tree that dates back to the origin of humankind.

Since most of us are busy with our present-day lives, we often do not think about the complexities of these interrelationships. If we use the approach of systems thinking and look at the big picture, we may find ways to understand these complexities and make our lives better. To go back to earlier examples, if we do not talk on the phone while driving, there could be fewer traffic accidents. If we can understand our genetic arrangement we have inherited from our ancestors, we might be able to find diseases to which we are susceptible. Therefore, systems thinking helps us see the interrelationships among things rather than linear cause-effect chains and see processes of change rather than snapshots.[4]

## Chapter 11: Krishna's Leadership Lessons

- The magnificence of the *Virat Rupa* symbolizes the discipline of systems thinking. Systems thinking is important for leadership as it helps to establish the framework of relationships rather than standalone objects or things, to see patterns rather than static snapshots.

- The supreme vision of the Virat Rupa symbolizes the strategic vision. Systems thinking enables leaders to think strategically and to see the big picture.

# 12

## *Leadership Commitment*

## Unselfish Commitment

Generally, we are driven by our needs and wants. Our commitment comes from the expectations we have to fulfill these needs and wants. We have expectations to earn our livelihood and to take care of our responsibilities. We have expectations to enhance our lives and the lives of those whom we love and for whom we care. These expectations lead us to become committed to our works and actions. The level of commitment also depends on the level of our expectations. The higher the expectation we have, the higher the commitment we have.

Social scientists have presented the *expectancy-valence theory* to suggest that individuals become committed only when the following three conditions exist:

1.  Higher levels of commitment that lead to higher performance;

2.  Better performances that lead to recognition and reward;

3.  Rewards obtained are for perceived needs and wants.[1]

The expectancy-valence theory applies to most people who do not think beyond rewards in concert with perceived needs and wants. Effective leaders, on the other hand, do not limit themselves to rewards for perceived needs and wants. They think beyond these boundaries, of enduring values that create continuous or perpetual fulfillment of needs and wants. Moreover, enduring values cannot be attained with selfish and self-centered commitment. It requires unselfish and unwavering commitment.

The leadership of Mandela attests to the fact that great and effective leaders operate with unselfish and unwavering commitment, a commitment that fosters enduring values that exceed ordinary needs and wants. Mandela's struggle against South African apartheid was a very long journey, one of the longest leadership challenges faced by a leader in the recent history. As a young ward working for the chief of Thembuland, he had observed the deprivations of his people. As a young lawyer, he fought for the rights of his clients, mostly the oppressed South Africans. However, he did not confine his commitment to his practice as a lawyer. With his leadership role in the ANC, he saw an opportunity to achieve higher and enduring values—the freedom of his people on a larger scale. He committed himself to fulfilling the higher needs and wants of his people, which were more important to him than were his own personal needs and wants.

Mandela was imprisoned for twenty-seven years. During his prison life, he never compromised his principles. He continued to reinforce his commitment to fight apartheid. He repeatedly turned down offers to be released from prison in exchange of compromises. When he was finally released from the prison in 1990, Mandela continued with his commitment for a free South Africa. In 1991, apartheid was revoked by then South African President F. W. de Clark. In 1994, elections were held, and Mandela was elected the president of the new and free South Africa.[2]

In the Bhagavad Gita, Krishna also reinforces the necessity of leadership commitment, a commitment to lead for enduring values. Krishna says, "Knowledge and understanding are better than rituals and practices. Meditation is better than knowledge and understanding. Renunciation of results is even better as it provides immediate harmony" (12:12).

Rituals and practices are learning processes. They enable us to become knowledgeable. The ancient Vedic texts describe the mortal life as a series of rituals and practices to obtain ultimate knowledge, the knowledge of the supreme consciousness.

Moreover, meditation is more important than knowledge. Why is meditation more important than knowledge? Because, according to the Bhagavad Gita and the Vedic texts, meditation is a powerful tool that brings us closer to our supreme consciousness. The meaning of mediation in the leadership context, as discussed in chapter 6, centers on the leader's ability to focus and stay on course of the vision and goals. Beyond this leadership focus, the renunciation of results leads to greater outcomes, as we have learned from the life of Mandela. Mandela understood that achieving freedom for his people was the right vision for his leadership role. Through a resilient commitment and focus that lasted for decades—including a twenty-seven-year prison sentence—Mandela was able to bring about a transforming change in South Africa. Neither the presidency of South Africa nor the Nobel Peace Prize was his final reward. His final reward was a place in the hearts of South Africans who longed for freedom.[3]

## Compassionate Leadership

In a world full of conflicts and adversity, today's leaders are faced with the dilemma to use force and retaliation as the primary tools of leadership. To fight off adversity, many leaders show a commitment toward aggression and conceit. Most of the time, the general perception of an effective leader is someone tough and aggressive. In general, leaders are expected to have more masculine traits than feminine traits. However, according to the Bhagavad Gita, leadership is about being single-minded with a vision and goals, not aggression or physical toughness. Rather than use force and retaliation, leaders need peace and compassion for their primary tools of leadership.

Compassionate leadership surpasses any other type of leadership. Pope John Paul II, Gandhi, Dr. King, and Mother Teresa demonstrated compassionate leadership and left lasting marks on humankind. When leaders lead with compassion, they spread emotions in positive ways. They inspire people by their optimism or compassion, which point toward a hopeful future. Force and aggression should always be secondary tools. Leaders should always show a commitment by demonstrating peace and compassion toward people and organizations. Like in Mahabharata, force should be utilized only when peace and compassion cannot work.

Although the battle of Kurukshetra was an overriding episode of the epic of Mahabharata and the Bhagavad Gita, one should not forget that many years were spent by the Pandavas and Krishna to make peace with the Kauravas. They had withstood humiliation and self-sacrifice before succumbing to the thought of a war. The Kauravas had attempted to kill the Pandavas by setting their palace on fire. They also forced the Pandavas to live thirteen years in exile. Krishna tried to bring peace by facilitating negotiations between the feuding families. Nonetheless, the Kauravas were adamant about taking away the rights of the Pandavas, who had no other choice but to stand up against the oppression of the Kauravas.

Referring to the compassionate leadership style, Krishna says, "The wise ones are friendly and compassionate and are not capable of ill will. They are devoid of selfish desires. With these attributes, they are close to the supreme consciousness" (12:13–14). Compassion and unselfish desires lead to a lasting leadership legacy. Compassionate leaders inspire people and disseminate rays of hope amid conflicts and adversity. The lives and leadership of Pope John Paul II, Carter, Gandhi, Dr. King, Mother Teresa, and Mandela all prove that compassionate leadership lasts longer than the leadership of one person's lifetime. Compassionate leaders become immortal through their legacies.

## Emotional Maturity

Krishna also suggests that a true leadership commitment comes from emotional maturity on the leaders' part. He notes, "Wise are those who are free from fear and anger and those who do not cause fear and anger in others" (12:15). Negative emotions such as anger and fear disrupt and distract our focus from important tasks. Anger or fear may get a leader through the crisis of the day, but they are short-lived motivators.[4] Aggressive and authoritarian leadership styles are driven by fear and anger. However, negative emotions that trigger fear and anger do not create leadership legacy. Anger and fear always lead to destructive emotions and behaviors, which may not be beneficial to people and organizations. Pol Pot, Hitler, Saddam Hussein, and Slobodan Milosevic were some authoritarian leaders who led by fear and anger. The world knows about the consequences of their leadership, and the world is still plagued by authoritarian leaders.

In the business world, an authoritarian leadership style translates to aggressive goals based solely on financial performance. Their goals hold little or no regard for organizational and individual well-being. Unfair treatment of employees, customers, and communities with a high level of awareness for personal benefits is an atypical combination of aggressive leadership styles. The leadership of Dunlap (a.k.a. Chainsaw Al) was an authoritarian style of leading businesses.

Speaking further on emotional maturity, Krishna says, "The wise ones neither crave for prosperity, nor do they run away from adversity. They are even-minded in prosperity and adversity" (12:17). This should not be misinterpreted as effective leaders spurn prosperity. They crave for the prosperity of their people and organization instead of only their own. Furthermore, leaders require personal strength and effectiveness to endure adversity. True and effective leaders rise at times of adversity. Dr. King once said, "The ultimate measure of a man is not where he stands in moments of comfort and convenience, but where he stands during challenges and controversy."

To become even-minded at all times, leaders need to look at prosperity and adversity in positive ways. They first need to accept that prosperity and adversity are fundamental to any life experience. Leaders must be able to channel negative events and emotions in a way that creates positive outcomes, especially when they deal with adverse situations. They need to embrace a rational way of thinking that promotes compassion and harmony among people and their organizations. When leaders know that prosperity and adversity must be handled with equanimity, they not only demonstrate emotional maturity; they also plant the seed of an enduring strength in their organizations.

## Chapter 12: Krishna's Leadership Lessons

- Effective leadership requires unselfish, unwavering commitment to achieve the common vision and goals of an organization.

- Compassionate leadership produces a positive and lasting legacy.

- Compassionate leaders are those full of love and respect for others and devoid of ill will and selfish desires.

- Effective leaders do not lead by fear or anger.

- Emotional maturity is very important to become effective leaders. Emotional maturity helps leaders handle prosperity and adversity in equanimity.

- Emotional maturity also helps leaders to stay focused on leadership commitments.

# 13

## *Self and Surroundings*

# Environmental Awareness

In this chapter, Krishna speaks on the importance of understanding our physical and psychological makeup and its relationship to our surroundings. "The great ones know what we are made up of—our basic physical composition as it relates to this physical world, and the dynamics of our senses, mind, and intellect. They know where pains and pleasures arise, and they know how to handle them" (13:1–8).

The understanding of physical and psychological composition is not necessarily about knowing our mind and body in great detail. The key is to understand the overall relationship between mind, body, and the environment. The human body is made up of five essential elements—earth, water, fire, air, and space (13:4), as follows:

*Earth:* If we look at the chemical composition of our body, we find chemicals like carbon, phosphorus, potassium, magnesium, iron, and many other elements. These elements are also found abundantly in the earth.

*Water:* The human body is made up of 60 to 70 percent water. Water is found in blood plasma, as well as lymph and cellular fluids. If we look at the earth's surface, about the same percent—70 percent—is covered with water.

*Fire:* The human body functions with the help of vital energy, which is mostly derived from food. The earth derives energy from the sun.

*Air:* The earth's atmosphere is filled mostly with nitrogen and oxygen. Oxygen is important to the human body. Nitrogen is important to plants, which produce oxygen for animal species.

*Space:* Space is the infinite vastness in which everything is located. Although we are sheltered by the earth's atmosphere, the earth and everything on it are contained in the infinite space.

In chapter 3, there was a discussion of the dynamics of senses, mind, and intellect. Our psychological setup is connected to our senses and mind. Whatever we perceive with our senses, we transport these messages from our senses to our mind. Our intellect is the ability to rationalize things, objects, and events. We also have the ability to translate the messages from our mind and intellect into actions. When this mind-body transaction happens, the Bhagavad Gita suggests that we have to be aware of our environmental surroundings the earth in general. Why? An awareness is needed because our environmental surroundings and their effects on the mind and body create human conditions.

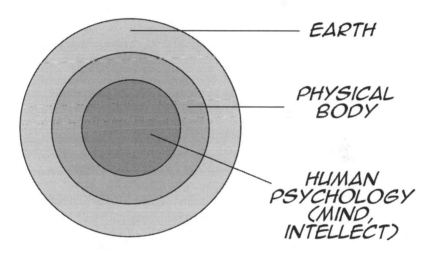

EARTH

PHYSICAL BODY

HUMAN PSYCHOLOGY (MIND, INTELLECT)

Relationship among mind, body, and earth

By understanding the relationship between and among the three essential factors—mind, body, and surroundings—we can understand the cause and effect of pain and pleasure, the two most basic human emotions. Creating a balanced relationship between and among these three factors helps us understand where and why emotions arise. By understanding the cause, we enhance our experience by controlling the effects.

For example, if we do something that requires intense thinking, the room temperature we are in has to be right for our body. If the room temperature is too cold or too hot, we cannot focus on our thoughts. If the room is too cold, drinking a warm cup of tea or adding one more layer of cloth usually helps warm our body; so we can focus on our thinking. If the room is too hot, a fan or an air cooler makes us more comfortable, which helps us to think comfortably. Therefore, by understanding this relationship, we can control, to some extent, the causes and effects of activities that require thinking. We can choose to be in a room with the right temperature. Alternatively, we can control other variables to influence these senses, such as warm tea or a fan, which help us cope with the room temperature.

The relationship among mind, body, and environment has an important meaning to leadership. Leaders need to think beyond people and organizations, and they must also think about the interests of their physical surroundings. The physical surroundings mainly refer to the earth or environmental conditions, which, in turn, influence human and organizational conditions. Environmentally conscious leaders strive to create healthy settings for their people and organizations, so everyone enjoys a healthy life experience. Physical and psychological growth become inevitable when the surrounding environment is healthy.

In the business world, corporate social responsibility is similar to the mind-body-earth relationship. "Corporate social responsibility is a commitment to improve community well-being through discretionary business practices and contributions of corporate resources," [1] says Philip Kotler in his book *Corporate Social Responsibility.* Corporate social responsibility advocates the use of business resources to meet the expectations of people, communities, and the environment. Today, more and more businesses are showing a commitment to enhance human conditions by investing in communities and the natural environment.

## Circle of Influence

Krishna says, "The wise ones are those who prefer solitude and do not follow the crowd. By remaining in solitude they seek for the ultimate knowledge that unites them with the supreme consciousness" (13:10). Solitude does not necessarily mean that one needs to be lonely and secluded all the time. Interaction with people is very important, especially for leaders. They should never be isolated from the people. With this consideration, the central message of the discourse is that leaders should always be selective in their circle of influence. When they are not dealing with the people and their circle of influence, leaders should seek quietness and solitude where they can engage in introspection and focus on things that matter most for them, their people, and their organizations.

The circle of influence is about surrounding ourselves with great people—people who influence us with positive energy, intelligence, peace, compassion, and confidence. The circle of influence is important for leaders as their effectiveness is largely determined by those who surround them. If the people around them radiate negative energy and are unintelligent, cruel, and uncaring, leaders will be unable to lead effectively or generate transforming changes.

Great leaders see their circle of influence as people who can enhance their strengths and correct their weaknesses. First, they analyze their own strengths and weaknesses. Second, leaders balance their weaknesses with the strengths of others; they surround themselves with competent people.

In chapter 2, the concept of having the right people on one's team and the wrong people off the team was discussed. The approach of creating the right circle of influence is the same: creating a good circle of influence is not only a recognition and acceptance of the right people; it includes staying away from the wrong people.

How do we know the right and wrong people? The Vedic texts suggest that we should choose our circle of influence by embracing people with a positive outlook on physical, psychological, and spiritual aspects of life. Creating the right circle of influence means examining the following important qualities in our associations with people:

*Physical well-being:* When we embrace people who are aware of their physical well-being, we are likely to be persuaded or motivated to become aware of our own physical well-being. A healthy diet and exercise habits help us avoid health problems. A sound physical health enhances our self-confidence and self-esteem in everyday life. In the ancient East, people practiced *Hatha Yoga* (physical exercise) to enhance their physical well-being.

*Psychological well-being:* People who thrive for mental strength seek good psychological health. Good psychological health helps us become better human beings and enhances the lives of people around us. By affiliating with people who are conscious of positive psychological development, we enrich ourselves with more knowledge and wisdom. Sound psychological well-being also helps us to tackle adversity with skill. In the ancient times, meditation was one of the traditional methods to enhance psychological development. People also followed *gurus* (enlightened teachers) to seek knowledge and wisdom.

*Spiritual well-being:* Spirituality is the core of our value system. We derive life's guidance and values from it. All spiritual traditions promote compassion, peace, and welfare of living beings and the earth. When we embrace spiritual people, we fill our lives with peace and compassion.

Today's technologically advanced society provides us with many tools and avenues to enrich our life experience. Television, video games, and the Internet are some tools most of us become captivated with, especially when we are not interacting with people. Sometimes, even social events are spun around activities such as watching television events, playing videogames, and engaging in interactions over the Internet. Although we may feel that these tools are enhancements for life, we do not realize that obsession with these tools is also a distraction. They take away the necessary and precious time for introspection. The meaning of solitude, as advised by Krishna, is merely reducing unnecessary distractions of life and spending time to look into our inner selves.

---

# Gandhi and His Circle of Influence

Mahatma Gandhi was a charismatic and an inspiring leader who led millions of followers and admirers in India and abroad. As he led India against the British rule, he was always in a company of an important circle of influence. Here are some of the many people who were key members of his circle of influence.

**Kasturba Gandhi:** She was the wife of Gandhi for sixty-two years. Kasturba was his moral strength and a close comrade in his struggle. She played a key role to lead the women in the fight against the British rule and to uplift the socially deprived groups. She took up the leadership role whenever Gandhi was arrested, and she was also jailed several times during the freedom campaign.

**Vallabhai Patel:** Popularly known as "Sardar" Patel, Patel is given credit for the integration of smaller traditional kingdoms into the union of India. (Sardar means chief or leader.) He was a great administrator; he held public positions before and after the independence of India. As a public administrator, Patel always fought for the rights of the poor peasants.

**Jawaharlal Nehru:** During the freedom fight, Nehru grew as Gandhi's protégé. His speeches, books, and letters demonstrate his ability as a great communicator. After he became the first prime minister of the independent India, Nehru pioneered many foreign policies that gave India a unique place in the world. He institutionalized democracy during his tenure as the prime minister.

**Mohammad Ali Jinnah:** Jinnah made significant contributions to the independence by leading Muslims in the fight against the British rule of India. Jinnah was a close ally to Gandhi until he led to the formation of the separate Muslim nation of Pakistan. He is best known as the father of Pakistan.

## Learning Paths

By looking into our inner selves, we can better understand our inner consciousness, which leads us to the supreme knowledge and wisdom. Solitude helps in this journey to the inner self. Krishna suggests three paths of yoga to attain the supreme goals of life. Yoga is the practice and discipline of controlling body and mind. "To attain the supreme consciousness, some follow the practice of meditation (*dhyana yoga*), some follow the path of continuous learning (*jnâna yoga*), and others follow the path of selfless service (*karma yoga*)" (13:25).

*Dhyana yoga:* Dhyana is the Sanskrit word for meditation. In a leadership context, dhyana yoga is the practice of focusing on vision and goals, which is also about looking into the inner self and understanding one's purpose and responsibilities toward other people.

*Jnâna yoga:* Jnâna is the Sanskrit word for knowledge. The path of jnâna yoga advocates that a leader learns from texts and teachers. It involves an intellectual approach of learning about the self, the surrounding environment, and the relationship between the two. Jnâna yoga leads to knowledge and wisdom.

*Karma yoga:* The Sanskrit meaning of karma is "deed or act." It also means cause and effect. Karma yoga is the path of selfless service. A leader who practices karma yoga thinks less of personal benefits and more of the fulfillment of the common good. This kind of yoga requires a leader to remove himself from the bondage of *I, me,* and *mine,* and to think in terms of working for a common cause. Karma yoga also calls for a leader to concentrate on actions and not become attached to outcomes. As Krishna advises in chapter 2, we have the right over our responsibilities and proper actions required of it; however, we do not have the rights to the rewards (2:47).

These three paths of yoga provide an important framework for leaders. Although every leadership situation can be unique, leaders can apply one or all of these paths in their leadership undertakings.

## Recognizing People's Potential

Krishna says, "The wise ones see and treat everyone with equality and justice" (13:28). Although leadership positions are held above all other positions in an organization's structure, effective leaders see themselves as the most responsible figures in a horizontal field rather than in a hierarchical pyramid. With compassion toward people, leaders see everyone in their organization as agents of growth and potential who contribute toward the organizational vision and goals. They consider leadership as a way to bring the best out of each individual instead of simply making them followers.

Fair treatment of people gives way to open communication and healthy relationships between leaders and followers. In politics, fair treatment of people promotes democratic values. In businesses, it promotes both top-down and bottom-up management styles: authority and power flow from top to bottom while support and actions flow from bottom to the top.

Today, more and more organizations acknowledge that one of the primary roles of leadership is the identification of potential leaders and the development of their leadership skills. This task is impossible without leaders acknowledging the potential of everyone in their organizations.

---

### Chapter 13: Krishna's Leadership Lessons

- Leaders need to think beyond people and organizations and also think in the interest of their physical surroundings. In the context of contemporary leadership, this awareness relates to issues such as environmental awareness and corporate social responsibilities.

- Leaders must surround themselves with the right circle of influence. The circle of influence is about surrounding ourselves with great people, people who radiate positive energy, intelligence, peace, compassion, and confidence.

- Effective leaders learn by three main paths: the practice of focus or meditation (dhyana yoga), the practice of continuous learning (jnâna yoga), and the practice of selfless service (karma yoga).

- Effective leaders treat everyone with equality and justice.

# 14
## *Leadership Character*

# Leadership Character

In the discourses of the Bhagavad Gita, Krishna repeatedly talks about human character, which is core to leadership effectiveness. Today, character is as important as it was in the times of Krishna and Arjuna.

According to the *American Heritage Dictionary*, character is the combination of qualities or features that distinguish one person, group, or thing from another.[1] A leader's character determines his or her potential, interpersonal skills, and the overall leadership role in an organization. In general, we refer to good character as the qualities one should have to be a virtuous and respected individual.

Various studies have shown that effective leadership character should incorporate the following important qualities:

- Integrity and honesty
- Focus on people
- Competence
- Vision and inspiration

Other important qualities include the following:

- Intelligence and decisiveness
- Caring and compassion
- Courage
- Dependability
- Dedication
- Openness to equality and justice

In chapter 7, Krishna explains to Arjuna the three main types of character, namely, sattvic, rajasic, and tamasic. In this chapter, Krishna discusses character in greater detail: "Sattvic is the character of purity and harmony;

rajasic is the character of compulsive growth and activity; tamasic is the character of ignorance and recklessness" (14:5).

"Sattvic character builds happiness. Rajasic builds compulsive actions, and tamasic builds ignorance" (14:9).

Sattvic leaders are driven by the harmony between the self and the surroundings. They long for neither their own suffering nor the suffering of others. At the same time, sattvic leaders also do not hesitate to accept suffering if such hardship begets peace and harmony for the people in their organizations.

Rajasic leaders, driven by compulsion and desires, do not hesitate to put people in pain and suffering. To accomplish selfish goals, they do not hesitate to sacrifice peace and harmony of their people.

Tamasic leaders are led by the needs of their five senses. They fail to use their intellect properly; hence, they are always in darkness and ignorance. They are driven by the need to delight their five senses. They do not realize the need for higher levels of consciousness. Their acts and choices are driven by ignorance and without a concern for others. Tamasic leaders, therefore, create chaos and darkness in their organizations.

What do the deeds of each character lead to? "The rewards of sattvic deeds are harmony and happiness. The rewards of rajasic deeds are pain and agony. The rewards of tamasic deeds are ignorance and unawareness" (14:16). Krishna further notes, "Knowledge and wisdom come from sattvic character. Selfish desires come from rajasic character. Ignorance and chaos arise from tamasic character" (14:17).

Good deeds nourish the self and the surroundings. Hence, they lead to knowledge and wisdom. Selfish deeds lead to pain and agony, and ignorant deeds lead to pitfalls and darkness. Anyone embarking on a leadership journey can introspect on these lessons and develop the right qualities to build a good character, the sattvic character. The goal of effective leadership is to create peace and happiness, knowledge and wisdom. Every leader should strive to become a sattvic leader. The following sections further examine Krishna's lessons on the three types of leadership character.

## Sattvic Leadership

"Sattvic character radiates calmness, purity, and righteousness. It embodies happiness and knowledge," says Krishna (14:6). Effective leadership character should incorporate integrity and focus on people and competency. Sattvic character radiates these qualities. It presents hope and inspiration to the people.

Studies conducted across the globe have shown that honesty is the number one quality that people expect in a leader. Honesty provides an important dimension to leadership. It creates credibility and trustworthiness. Today, many leaders struggle with credibility because they have shown themselves to be dishonest and deceitful. Many leaders lure their followers with hefty promises only to be forgotten once they capture their leadership positions. Many leaders promise prosperity only to lose focus on people and their well-being.

Leaders should always focus on people and demonstrate compassion toward them. Leadership is not about leaders; it is about people and organizations. Putting the interest, needs, and wants of the people before personal agendas builds leadership character.

Leaders should also be inspirational, so their followers can have hope and gain inspiration from them. Leaders inspire by becoming teachers and through their commitment to shared values and principles. Buddha, Jesus, Mohammad, and Krishna were teacher-leaders. Some inspire by becoming heroes devoting themselves to great causes and noble works. Christopher Columbus, Charles Darwin, and Henry Ford were hero-leaders devoted to great causes. Some leaders are charismatic by nature and inspire their followers by being great communicators. Dr. King, Gandhi, and Kennedy were charismatic leaders who inspired people by communicating elegantly.[2]

Competence is another quality that gives leadership credibility. A leader's capability and track record are instruments of motivation for followers. One cannot proclaim himself as a leader without proven capability and track record. To become an effective leader, one must be experienced in adverse and prosperous situations. By managing adverse situations, leaders can demonstrate their true character.

Honesty, integrity, compassion, motivation, and competence are pillars of trust for leaders. When leaders are trustworthy, their followers believe in the vision and goals they present for their organizations. James Kouzes and Barry Posner say in their book *The Leadership Challenge*, "If you don't believe in the messenger, you won't believe the message."[3]

The central leadership message of the Bhagavad Gita is to become a sattvic leader. Krishna emphasizes sattvic leadership and suggests that every leader should build sattvic character. By becoming an honest, trustworthy, compassionate, competent, and inspiring leader, one can transform any organization and lead people through the worst of adversities and the best of prosperities.

Sattvic leadership also requires a leader to ward off rajasic and tamasic qualities. Selfish desires, compulsive actions, inactivity, ignorance, and unnecessary indulgence must always be avoided. Instead, by developing sattvic qualities, a leader should focus on people and selfless service.

## Rajasic Leadership

Krishna says, "Rajasic character builds selfish desires and attachments, which leads to uncontrollable actions" (14:7). Krishna does not say to go without desires. Rather, he suggests that desires should be based on the common good rather than on selfish interests. Self-centered desires and attachments are not what leaders should harness because the consequences of such desires and attachments may ultimately be unfavorable to leadership and their organizations.

Today, we hear about many leadership situations that depict vivid examples of selfish desires on leaders' parts. Some leaders prefer hoarding power, authority, and other personal benefits. To achieve their selfish goals, they become authoritarians and autocrats. They do not hesitate to put their people in pain and agony to fulfill their own personal needs. Some even engage in brutality and killing to meet these personal goals.

In the business world, financial incentives for many business leaders are based on aggressive business goals that focus less on customers and workers than on the bottom line. In highly competitive industries, customers and workers suffer because many leaders act with selfish desires and attachments. Many have led their organizations to debacle, simply because they focused on selfish desires instead of the interests of their stakeholders.

When leaders act with selfish desires, they disseminate negative energy to their people and throughout their organizations. This negative energy can manifest itself in the form of pain or agony, or it can also be in the form of bad influence. Selfish leaders also have the potential to create selfish followers. Krishna says, "Rajasic character promotes greed and restlessness" (14:12). A selfish and greedy leader also encourages similar behavior among the people. When people are led by a selfish leader, they are inclined to follow their leader's attitude simply to survive in the organization. Some followers may choose to follow the selfish leader because of the stability and security the organization offers. Some may follow selfish leaders because of the status and recognition that such allegiance to a selfish leader confers.

Rajasic leadership, therefore, creates rajasic followership. Rajasic followership is about pleasing the selfish leader for his or her selfish desires or acting without any regard to other people and the surroundings. Corruption, violence, and inhumane acts are atypical of organizations ruled by rajasic leaders and filled with rajasic followers. An organization filled with rajasic people does not befriend peace and happiness.

# Tamasic Leadership

According to Krishna, "Ignorance, sluggishness, and indulgence result from tamasic character" (14:8). Tamasic leaders act without knowledge, wisdom, and compassion. They do what they please and do not think about their actions and the consequences. They are never proactive; and when they engage in an action, they usually overdo what is required of the action.

"When tamasic character becomes dominant, a person's life is filled with darkness, chaos, and confusion" (14:13). Ignorance ultimately leads to chaos and confusion. Ignorance on leaders' part leads to mismanagement and incompetence.

Incompetent leaders lack experience, knowledge, and expertise. The danger lies in leaders' ignorance of their incompetence. They believe they are capable and act without knowledge and intelligence. Incompetence also arises from a lack of potential or an ability to focus. By refusing to learn and to act, leaders become stagnant and dormant, which, in turn, leads their organizations to become the same.

---

## Chapter 14: Krishna's Leadership Lessons

- Character is core to effective leadership.

- An effective leader should develop *sattvic* character.

- Sattvic leadership means leading with honesty, integrity, trustworthiness, compassion, and competence.

- Sattvic character gives credibility to leaders.

- Leaders should avoid leading with *rajasic* or *tamasic* qualities.

---

# 15

*The Ultimate Wisdom*

# Tree of Wisdom

In chapter 15, Krishna discusses a unique tree called the *ashvatha* tree, also known as the banyan tree, which is only found in tropical Asia and Pacific islands. The banyan tree has an unusual shape. Its roots develop from its branches; some of the roots descend toward the earth and become trunks. It also has large, oval leaves and cherry-like fruits that are a favorite to birds and animals.

A full-grown banyan tree becomes a collection of dense roots and trunks that spread over a large area. Over many years, it becomes difficult to locate the main trunk from the assortment of trunks that have grown from the branches of its original trunk. The banyan tree can grow up to 30 meters tall. The largest reported banyan tree is in Calcutta, India, with a main trunk of 13 feet in diameter, and with 230 large trunks and 3,000 smaller ones. Another member of the *Ficus* family—*Ficus religiousa,* which is popularly known as the pipal tree—is believed to be the tree under which Siddhartha Gautama received enlightenment and became the Buddha.

Pointing to the unique characteristics of the banyan tree, Krishna tells Arjuna, "The true essence of the ashvatha tree—its beginning and end—is not perceived in this world. The true understanding of this tree leads to the ultimate wisdom" (15:1–4). There is no established argument or explanation for the meaning of what a banyan tree signifies to human life. If Krishna talks about the banyan tree in the discourses of the Bhagavad Gita, there could be an interesting metaphorical meaning of this unique tree.

In *Srimad Bhagavad Gita,* Swami Chinmayananda gives his explanation of the metaphorical meaning of the banyan tree. The Sanskrit name *ashvatha* means "the ever-changing future." *A* is none; *shva* is future; *tha* is consistent. The main trunk of the banyan tree is the primary source of life. Roots that originate from the branches signify the origin from "above," meaning divinity. The roots protruding toward the earth suggest attachment with earthly elements. The leaves are the sense objects.[1] Most of its physiology is similar to other plants: with the process of photosynthesis, leaves consume light energy from the sun, water from the roots, and carbon dioxide from the air to produce sugar and oxygen.

Banyan Tree

What does the banyan tree signify in the context of leadership? In my opinion, the banyan tree signifies the concept of the *learning organization*, a concept introduced by Peter Senge in *The Fifth Discipline: The Art & Practice of the Learning Organization.* According to Senge, learning organizations are those organizations where people continually expand their capacity to create the results they truly desire, where new and expansive patterns of thinking are nurtured, where collective aspiration is set free, and where people are continually learning to see the whole together.[2]

Roots spread from the branches of a banyan tree and turn into new trunks. Compared to other trees, this metamorphosis is unique. The complexity of the structure is unique for each banyan tree. The entanglement of roots, branches, and leaves create a small forest in itself. Branches and leaves of most trees, in general, rely on the water and nutrients supplied from a single set of roots. The banyan tree, however, continuously spreads its structure forming new roots, trunks, and leaves. This expansion results in the increase of the total surface area of roots and leaves, which helps the tree absorb more water supply and nutrients from the roots—all of which aids in improved photosynthesis.

Like the banyan tree, a learning organization continually expands its capacity to create its future.[3] Peter Senge further says, "Through learning we re-create ourselves. Through learning, we become able to do something we never were able to do. Through learning, we re-perceive the world and our relationship to it. Through learning we extend our capacity to create, to be part of the generative learning process of life...."[4]

## Understanding the True Self

In chapter 7, Krishna suggests that we should know ourselves before leading others. We should know our strengths and weaknesses before promoting the strengths and correcting the weaknesses of others. In chapter 13, Krishna emphasizes learning our physical and psychological composition and their relationship to our physical surroundings. In this chapter, he further emphasizes understanding our true selves. He suggests that understanding our true self is an important part of finding the ultimate wisdom. Krishna says, "The ignorant do not see the self that resides in the body. They do not see the self nourishing from the senses or acting through character. But the wise ones see the true self" (15:10).

What is the self? The *American Heritage Dictionary* defines the word "self" as the consciousness of one's own being or identity.[5] In other words, the consciousness of one's being or identity is the awareness of one's physical and psychological states. I am tall or I am short. My complexion is fair or dark. My eyes are brown or blue. I am happy or sad. I am intelligent or unintelligent. These are all either physical or psychological awareness of the self.

Physical or psychological awareness comes from what is perceived by our senses. My sight tells me the height of my body relative to other people or things, so I know whether I am tall or short. I see my complexion relative to the complexion of other people or things, so I know whether my complexion is fair or dark. Emotions, such as happiness and sadness, and other perceptions of one's psychological capabilities like intelligence come from the interpretation or processing of messages by the brain. Emotions are also relative to other emotions; however, we usually do not compare our emotions with others'. We usually say we are sad, but we do not compare our sadness with others' sadness.

When we go to sleep, our senses are not as active as when we are awake. Therefore, the consciousness of our physical and psychological states declines during the sleeping hours. Sometimes, when we have physical pain, we do not feel it when we go to sleep. If the consciousness of the self declines during the sleeping hours, does the self lose its value and identity during sleep when the senses are not that active? The dictionary meaning of the self only makes sense if we are awake.

When we are in sleep or in coma, we refer to our consciousness as sub-consciousness or semi-consciousness. During sleep or coma, our senses still function well, but our level of cognition declines. In general, the states of full-consciousness, sub-consciousness, and semi-consciousness are, therefore, dependent on the cognition derived from our physical senses.

The ancient Vedic wisdom defines the consciousness of the self as not limited to our physical or psychological awareness. It teaches us other levels of consciousness that are not always dependent on our senses. It states that too much focus and dependency on our senses alienates us from exploring other levels of consciousness.

The ancient wisdom describes several states of consciousness, most of which are yet to be explored by science. These states of consciousness can be broadly categorized as follows:

*State of being awake:* In this state of consciousness, our senses interact with our brain. The awareness of the self is based on the cognition of our physical and psychological states as perceived by our senses and mind. This is the basic state of consciousness for human beings.

*Sleeping:* During sleep, our senses react to some stimuli; but our cognition and interactions are limited. Dreams take us to the next state of consciousness. In this state, we can see images and hear sounds; but those perceptions are not based on our physical senses. Sometimes we see distinct colors and hear distinct sounds in our dreams, which are not perceived by our senses but recorded in our memory in some way.

*Dhyana:* Dhyana is the state of meditation. When we meditate, we experience absolute peace that comes from our inner being. Scientific studies have revealed that this state has physiological connections as well. When people meditate, they usually experience a reduction of stress and an improvement in blood pressure.

*Inner consciousness:* The next state of consciousness is the innermost consciousness that governs over the physical existence. Many refer to this state as the *soul.* In this state of consciousness, physical consciousness becomes less significant. Recognition or experience of this state leads to enlightenment. Krishna, Buddha, Jesus, and Mohammed lived their lives with the awareness of inner consciousness.

*Supreme consciousness:* In the final state of consciousness, everything—physical and nonphysical things—merges into absolute oneness. Consciousness becomes universal, and this highest state of consciousness pervades everything. We refer to this consciousness as the Supreme Being.

This ancient wisdom suggests that the true self can only be realized when we acknowledge and understand all levels of consciousness. Our true self permeates throughout all levels of consciousness. The true self exists beyond the boundaries of physical life because the higher levels of consciousness are not limited to physical existence.

The true understanding of all levels of consciousness is not an easy task. So, how do we understand them? Krishna says, "Those who dedicate themselves on the path of yoga see the self within. The undisciplined and the doubtful fail to see the self within" (15:11).

In chapter 13, we discussed yoga as the practice and discipline of controlling mind and body. To understand the true self amid multiple layers of consciousness, one needs to practice the discipline of focus, self-awareness, and compassion.

The true understanding of the self is especially important for leaders if they wish to be effective. Understanding the true self becomes even more important for leaders as they are required not only to identify their own selves but to help others do the same as well. By understanding their true selves, leaders can explore their own potentiality. By helping others understand their true selves, leaders bring out the best in the people in their organizations.

## Supreme Consciousness

Krishna says, "There are two types of entities in this world: the perishable and the imperishable. The physical existence is perishable, and the higher consciousness is imperishable" (15:16). Within the levels of consciousness, we can notice a progression from physical or material existence to nonphysical existence. For human beings, physical existence has limitations. We are born and we die. However, the nonphysical existence has no such limitations. Nonphysical existence is not confined to birth and death.

The highest level of consciousness, the supreme consciousness, is without limitations and has absolute potential. Moreover, the supreme consciousness encompasses everything in this universe: "The supreme consciousness is indestructible. The supreme consciousness pervades everything" (15:17). What does this mean for leadership? Why did Krishna emphasize on the higher levels of consciousness?

One way to look at different levels of consciousness is by acknowledging that leaders should strive to lead with imperishable qualities and values—qualities and values of higher levels of consciousness. What are the imperishable qualities and values? What are perishable qualities and values? Krishna describes these in the next chapter.

## Chapter 15: Krishna's Leadership Lessons

- The uniqueness of the banyan tree symbolizes a learning organization. A learning organization continually expands its capacity to create its future.

- The true self can only be realized when we acknowledge and understand the different levels of consciousness.

- The understanding of the true self is important for leaders as they are required not only to identify their own selves but to help others do the same.

- Focusing on perishable or physical existence limits the power of leadership. Leaders should focus on values and qualities that are imperishable and long-lasting.

# 16

## *Divine and Diabolic Qualities*

# Divine Qualities

In previous chapters, Krishna discussed, for the most part, divine qualities. In this chapter, Krishna talks about divine and diabolic qualities. Below are some of the important divine qualities Krishna speaks about in the chapter (16:1–4).

*Fearlessness:* Arjuna needs courage to fight the battle of Kurukshetra. Krishna's discourses throughout the Bhagavad Gita raise Arjuna's courage and morale. Like Arjuna, leaders need courage to lead people through change and conflict. This courage is not just a momentary act of bravery; it is bravery over time. This courage is also about the willingness to risk for a positive change and to perform under stress.

Gandhi, Dr. King, and Mandela provided exemplary courage when they led their respective causes. They were defeated again and again, but they stood against their oppositions with firmness and determination. They were all jailed several times under harsh conditions. However, each time they were jailed or punished, they gathered more strength to fight against the forces that obstructed their values and principles.

*Purity of heart:* Purity of heart is not only to be gentle, kind, and loving. Purity means being true to the self and to others. For leaders, purity means being rational when it comes to the interests of people and the organization. Leaders need to acknowledge wholeheartedly that they are responsible for the welfare of their people and organizations. They need to learn that power, authority, and other incentives that come with leadership must be used for the benefit of the people first and foremost. By focusing on people and compassion toward them, leaders achieve purity of heart.

*Righteousness:* Righteousness is harmony with one's virtues and morality. Virtues and morality are usually influenced by traditional and cultural values, experience, and education. Effective leaders—whether political, community, or business leaders—need to be cognizant of their virtues and values. These fundamental virtues and values influence the intent, means, and consequences of moral behavior and other day-to-day conduct. Today, ethics is an important issue for leaders everywhere. Should we go to war or not? Should we curtail freedom to enforce discipline? Should we make profitability more important than customer satisfaction? Should we sacrifice the organization's future for immediate benefits? These are all ethical dilemmas faced by today's leaders.

When it comes to ethics, the Bhagavad Gita teaches leaders to lead with the highest degree of morality. Leaders leading with the highest degree of morality are concerned with right and wrong conduct over and above self-interest, apart from the views of others, and without regard to authority figures.[1] Great leaders like Gandhi, Dr. King, and Mother Teresa led with judgment and conduct based on the highest degree of morality.

*Charity:* The dictionary's definition of charity is the provision of help or relief to the poor.[2] Donations, contributions, and gifts are conventional forms of charity. Some individuals are charitable for fame or for personal benefits, such as tax breaks. Charity, in the context of leadership and as defined by the Bhagavad Gita, means more than donations and gifts. It means the genuine sense of giving to others. This giving is directed toward the happiness of the people and organization by fulfilling their needs and wants. Some of the many important aspects of leadership charity include the following:

- Charity is the act of putting the people's interest first.
- Sharing is another important act of charity. Whether for peace or economic profitability, people must have a share of whatever rewards an organization receives.

- Thinking of the long-term benefits of an organization is another act of charity. Leaders are not only responsible for the well-being of the organization in the present time but also for the future.

- Social responsibilities are other forms of charity. Social responsibility is the act of giving back to society and the community.

*Self-control:* Studies have shown that those who faced failure handled pressure poorly and were prone to moodiness and angry outbursts. Studies have also shown that the successful stayed composed under stress, remaining calm and confident. Leaders who have control over their emotions and actions not only become good decision makers, they also present themselves as trustworthy and dependable people—two of the main qualities followers seek in leaders.

*Selfless service:* Working without the motive of personal benefits, self-interest, and affiliation is selfless service. Selfish desires are the opposing force of effective leadership. A leader who is worried only about his own benefits can never be truly effective. Effective leadership is not about the livelihood of leaders; it is about the livelihood of everyone within the organization. Effective leaders are concerned about everyone in their organizations; so whatever they do, they act on behalf of everyone and for the benefit of everyone. This is selfless service.

*Trust in scriptures:* Scriptures are the ancient texts of wisdom. The Bible, Koran, the *Upanishads*, and *Tao-te-Ching* are examples of scriptures. Every scripture teaches about compassion, courage, integrity, selfless service, personal effectiveness, emotional awareness, and other virtues. Today, we may be well versed with the contemporary theories and practices of personal effectiveness. However, if we look closely, these theories and practices find their origins in the fundamental values and principles taught by scriptures.

*Renunciation:* Many misinterpret renunciation as simply renouncing or giving up everything they have, including tangible and intangible things and objects. They believe that one has to give up earthly possessions and desires for renunciation. The true meaning of renunciation is not giving up everything, but acknowledging that earthly possessions and virtuous desires are intended to make life meaningful. These possessions and desires need to be utilized properly to attain higher goals of life. The higher goals are for the common good rather than for personal benefits only.

Renunciation is the most challenging aspect of leadership. Leaders use renunciation of authority, power, and other privileges to make the lives of the people better. Leaders need to acknowledge that the leadership privileges are not intended to make their own personal lives better; rather, they are intended to be used for the benefit of all the people and organizations.

The leadership of Pope John Paul II is an example of leadership renunciation. He held a prominent leadership position at the Vatican, with authority, power, and privileges that came with the papal position. He was the central figure for more than one billion Catholics around the world. Yet, he reached out to people across all borders, beliefs, and cultures. He became a symbol of hope, peace, and happiness. He used his position of leadership to empower people and to make them happy. Empowering people is an act of leadership renunciation.

The Dalai Lama is another leader who has dedicated his life for peace and happiness of people of all beliefs and traditions. He comes from the Buddhist tradition, yet his teachings on peace and harmony have empowered people throughout the whole world and across all beliefs and cultures.

*Absence of anger, malice, and pride:* Every human being is susceptible to anger, malice, and pride. However, effective leaders make themselves aware of these emotions and suppress these emotions to lead effectively. Emotions like anger and malice may get a leader through the crisis of the day, but they are short-lived motivators. Pride generates selfish thoughts and desires. Pride prevents leaders from thinking about the interest of the people and organizations. Effective leaders should exercise equanimity at all times.

*Compassion:* Compassionate leadership promotes equality and fairness among the people. It helps leaders realize the true potential of people. Compassionate leaders are successful in leaving a lasting legacy, as they are able to inspire their people and create hope amid conflicts and adversity. The lives and leadership of Pope John Paul II, Carter, Gandhi, Dr. King, Mother Teresa, and Mandela prove that compassionate leadership lasts longer than a given leader's tenure.

*Perseverance:* Effective leadership does not happen overnight. Effective leadership grows out of a strong determination over a long period of time. Mandela was imprisoned for twenty-seven years. Even after his release in 1990, he continued to fight against South African apartheid. Dr. King was involved in the civil rights movement as early as the 1950s. He was still fully involved in the movement until the day of his assassination in 1968. Gandhi led his first mass meeting against the British rule in 1906. It took him and India more than four decades of hard work to gain independence from the British. Great leadership requires perseverance.

# Diabolic Qualities

Krishna cautions against some of the diabolical qualities as well, as noted below (16:4–24).

*Hypocrisy and dishonesty:* Krishna cautions against hypocrisy (16:4). Hypocrisy is the act of insincerity. It is the act of pretending to have certain values but not really following them in reality. Today, many leaders present themselves as hypocrites because they do not do what they promised to do or do what they never promised to do. They promise one thing in the beginning and do the opposite once they are in a position of author-ity. Hypocrites undertake actions that oppose the values and principles they once stood for. When leaders become hypocrites, they lose credibility, trustworthiness, and dependability. Followers can no longer look up to hypocrites for leadership.

Krishna also cautions against dishonesty (16:4). Cheating, lying, and deceit are forms of dishonest behavior. Dishonesty on a leader's part does not last long, as dishonest leaders eventually lose their credibility and trustworthiness.

*Pride and ego:* Krishna says, "Self-centered people thrive on power and money. They enjoy humiliating other people to make themselves look good" (16:14–15). Arrogance and ignorance lead to pride and ego. Lead-ers who fail to understand the real meaning of renunciation and compas-sion fall prey to pride and ego. Al Dunlap professed the effectiveness of his toughness as a key leadership tool. He took pride in his "chainsaw" method, which was to cut back costs and to fire employees. Later, analysis showed his cutback strategy was too costly and damaging to the companies for which he worked. Eventually, Al Dunlap invited his own defeat by being too proud and egocentric.

Leaders should develop some pride, but not the pride for their author-ity, position and privileges. Rather, they should be proud of the potential of their people and organizations. Pride and ego become positive forces when leaders disseminate a sense of belonging and a sense of achievement among people. At an organization level, that sense of pride usually trans-lates into loyalty toward the organization. At a national level, that sense of pride translates into nationalism and patriotism.

*Anger and cruelty:* Anger is a universal emotion to which everyone is sus-ceptible. Anger is an unpleasant emotion that generally results from injury, mistreatment, or opposition and usually results in a defense against the cause of that emotion. Anger can be appropriate and inappropriate.[3] Appropriate anger leads to correcting a wrong behavior such as social oppression and injustice. A lack of awareness usually gives rise to inappropriate anger. When we cannot properly rationalize the causes of anger, it becomes inappropriate. Furthermore, channeling anger in a destructive way leads to more anger and unpleasant situations. Aggression and cruelty are angry responses, which, in almost all cases, are inappropriate.

For leaders, using anger destructively means risking the tranquility of the people and organizations. People, especially leaders, must be emotionally aware of situations that make them angry. They need to understand the real causes of their anger and channel them in healthy ways. Anger needs to be handled with intelligence, and it should be channeled in constructive ways.

*Ignorance*: Ignorance is thinking and acting without virtue, knowledge, or awareness. When we are filled with ignorance, we tend to do what we should avoid and avoid the things we should do (16:7). Ignorance on an individual's part leads to confusion and chaos (16:16). Ignorance on a leader's part makes people and organizations vulnerable to failure and frustration. Leaders lose credibility if they do nothing to suppress their ignorance. Leaders who thrive for knowledge and wisdom gain credibility and a followership.

*Ruled by senses:* People who are inclined toward immorality see *kama* (sense gratification) as their highest goal (16:11). They cross many boundaries to fulfill their selfish desires (16:12). When it comes to leadership, being ruled by senses could make leaders extremely self-centered. Longing for sense gratification, they focus on things that bring pleasure to their senses. They long to see, hear, and feel good things. This sense gratification is not only for tangible and physical things. People ruled by their senses also prefer to hear praise with little regard to criticism. They desire to feel respected without gaining respect. Instead of serving and leading others, they become addicted to attention.

*Senseless giving:* Krishna said people with diabolic qualities "perform charity to swagger power and wealth" (16:17). Charity in the name of personal benefits is not really an act of true giving. Charity becomes senseless giving when it is intended for fame, expected returns, and other hidden agendas. When a gift is given for the sole benefit of the recipient with no expectations in return, then it becomes an act of true charity. Jack London writes in his essay *The Road,* "A bone to the dog is not charity. Charity is the bone shared with the dog when you are just as hungry."

Krishna says, "Unnecessary sensual desires, anger, and greed are three guaranteed ways to downfall. Those who can rid these three qualities can attain long-lasting success and happiness" (16:21–22). Effective leadership thrives when leaders can control their personal desires, anger, and greed. When they control these emotions, they can look beyond themselves and reach out to their people.

## Chapter 16: Krishna's Leadership Lessons

- Leaders need enduring courage. This courage is not just bravery of the moment, but bravery over time.

- By being true to the self and to others, leaders achieve purity of heart.

- Leaders need to lead with the highest degree of morality, which is righteous conduct over and above self-interest apart from the views of others and without regard to authority figures.

- A genuine sense of giving and service, without expecting anything in return, is the true leadership charity.

- Leaders with self-control become trustworthy and dependable.

- Leaders need to acknowledge that leadership privileges are not intended to make their own lives better. Rather, they are intended to be used for the benefits of their people and organizations.

- Effective leaders are always aware of their emotions and they maintain equanimity at all times.

- Effective leadership grows out of a strong determination over a long period of time.

- Effective leadership is devoid of hypocrisy, pride, ego, anger, cruelty, ignorance, and arrogance.

# 17

## *Sattvic Leadership*

## Sattvic Conviction

"Human nature is made up of faith. A person becomes whatever he believes in with faith," says Krishna (17:3). Faith here does not only signify traditional and spiritual beliefs; it signifies conviction. One's conviction could be based on traditional beliefs, but it can also be shaped up by other influences such as family, friends, and socioeconomic and environmental factors. A genuine conviction is one that is based on virtues and morality. For example, a true belief to fight against oppression for the common good is a genuine conviction. This is a sattvic conviction. A belief that takes away benefits of others for selfish desires is not a genuine or sattvic conviction.

Effective leadership cannot flourish without genuine convictions. Leaders who succeed to become authoritarians and dictators also have convictions, but their convictions are not genuine. Today, we know Gandhi, Dr. King, and Mandela as effective leaders because they all demonstrated genuine conviction. Authoritarian leaders like Hitler and Pol Pot had convictions, but they were not genuine.

Lord Buddha once said, "We are what we think. All that we are arises with our thoughts. With our thoughts we make the world." When we strongly reinforce our thoughts, they lead to intentions. When our intentions are strongly reinforced, they become convictions. A strong conviction later becomes a reality, as everything one does and every action one undertakes is based on that conviction. Effective leadership also starts with genuine thoughts, intentions, and conviction.

## Sattvic Discipline

Krishna said that there are three types of self-discipline to be practiced with conviction. This is the sattvic discipline (17:17). The three types of self-discipline are described below.

*1. The discipline of learning:* Krishna emphasizes the need to be learners, "Firm belief in teachers and people with wisdom— this is a self-discipline" (17:14). Krishna suggests that leaders have to learn from mentors who can teach values that can surpass leadership positions. They should learn from those who are experienced and learned and revere them with devotion.

Leadership becomes effective when there is a willingness not only to teach but also to learn. Leadership is not only about teaching people to follow a certain path or to do a certain thing. It is also about learning things that need to be taught. Effective leaders have to be effective learners.

*2. The discipline of speaking properly:* Krishna says, "To speak truly, gently, and without harsh words—this is another self-discipline" (17:15). Communication skills are very important for leaders to be effective. Effective leaders are effective in all forms of communication—reading, writing, speaking, and listening.

According to Krishna, the most important part of communication is to communicate with honesty and with respect toward others. For leaders to be effective, they must be able to motivate their followers when they speak, so they can guide them toward the vision and goals. Today, many leaders use harsh words against their opponents and enemies as a way to demonstrate their leadership conviction. They speak antagonistically to defeat or to oust their opponents. However, according to Krishna, this demagoguery is not a characteristic of effective leadership.

Gandhi spent his lifetime communicating effectively. He fought nonviolently against British rule in India. However, he never spoke harshly about the British. When he advocated for India's independence, he said, "We want the British to leave, but we want them to leave as friends."

*3. The discipline of equanimity:* Krishna said, "Calmness, gentleness, silence—these are the self-discipline of the mind" (17:16). The consistent practice of calmness and gentleness leads to perseverance. Being overtly excited in times of prosperity and overtly depressed in times of adversity cannot make a leader lead effectively. When one can think and act calmly at all times, the greatest of all challenges can be solved easily. Being calm promotes logical thinking. Actions undertaken with logical thinking always lead to more favorable outcomes.

Silence is not always about remaining quiet but focusing more on listening, observing, and thinking. We can act meaningfully when we can listen, observe, and think carefully. Although we get to see our leaders mostly when they are communicating to their followers, effective leaders spend significant time practicing calmness, gentleness, and silence.

## Sattvic Deeds

Honest, compassionate, competent, visionary, intelligent, courageous, trustworthy—all these traits are qualities of a sattvic leader, as described by Krishna. Along with these qualities, "a sattvic person performs actions with a firm belief in his or her responsibilities and without attachment to results" (17:11).

Before taking decisions and actions, leaders must have the right conviction for the desired vision and goals. To fulfill the vision and goals, leaders need to understand and acknowledge their responsibilities. Krishna emphasizes that leaders must be proactive in their accountability for their responsibilities and must delegate responsibilities to others. He also stresses that leaders need to motivate everyone to assume their responsibilities.

It is a great challenge to take up responsibilities and not become attached to the results. Generally, we get attached to the results when we have spent considerable time and effort on a task. If we work hard at our jobs, we expect a raise, promotion, or other recognitions. If we work hard on our projects, we expect the projects to be successful. However, Krishna had a unique lesson when it came to the association between hard work and results. Leaders should work hard without attachment to results because the leadership work is not intended to benefit leaders solely. The acts of leadership should benefit the people and organization more than the leaders themselves.

Effective leaders like Gandhi, Dr. King, and Pope John Paul II demonstrated that leadership can flourish without becoming attached to the results. Gandhi fought hard for the independence of India, but he did not expect to rule India after its independence. Instead, he supported other leaders like Jawaharal Nehru, Mohammad Jinnah, and Vallabhbhai Patel for key leadership positions. Dr. King fought hard for racial equality, not for personal benefits but for the civil rights of oppressed Americans. Pope John Paul II spent most of his papal tenure advocating for peace and friendship among the people of all nations and cultures. He did not expect anything in return for his advocacy for peace.

Krishna also speaks about two other types of deeds that are disparate to sattvic deeds. He notes that "a rajasic person performs actions for show and for selfish desires, and a tamasic person performs actions without regard for anyone and without good intentions" (17:12–13). The act of leadership for personal benefits with no consideration for other people is not a characteristic of effective leadership.

In this chapter, Krishna further emphasizes charity as a sattvic deed: "The act of giving without expecting anything in return, but with a good purpose is a sattvic charity. The act of giving with expecting something in return or unwillingness in giving is a rajasic charity. The act of giving without a good purpose, and in an inappropriate circumstance is a tamasic charity" (17:20–22).

Leaders become effective if they have a genuine sense of giving to others. They become true leaders when they can work hard for their people and organizations without expecting anything in return. And even if they do expect something in return for their charity, effective leaders should expect to receive the happiness of their people.

## Chapter 17: Krishna's Leadership Lessons

- Effective leaders have a genuine conviction for the common good of their people.

- Leadership is not only about teaching people to follow a certain path; it is also about learning things that need to be taught.

- When effective leaders communicate, they communicate with honesty and show respect to others.

- Effective leaders spend significant time practicing calmness, gentleness, and silence. Practicing these qualities makes them effective listeners, observers, and thinkers.

- Meaningful actions are created by careful thinking and careful observations.

- Leaders need the right conviction for the desired vision and goals of their organizations.

- Leaders should work hard without attachment to the results because the outcome of effective leadership should benefit the people and organizations more than the leaders themselves.

- Acts of leadership for personal benefits only and without consideration for others is not a characteristic of effective leadership.

- Effective leaders engage themselves in sattvic charity, a genuine sense of giving without expecting anything in return.

# 18

## *Renunciation—The Ultimate Leadership Challenge*

# The Meaning of Renunciation

When Arjuna listens to Krishna talk about renunciation in the previous discourses, he becomes more curious about the concept. He asks Krishna to further explain the meaning of renunciation.

"There are two types of renunciation. To abstain from selfish acts is called *sanyasa*, and to detach from the results of an action is *tyaga*" (18:2).

Renunciation is not necessarily about giving up material possessions and desires. It is about acknowledging that material possessions and desires are intended to make life meaningful and that these possessions and desires need to be utilized properly to attain higher and meaningful goals in life.

The perceived meaning of sanyasa is reflected by the word *sanyasi*, commonly known in the East as people who have given up earthly possessions and sensual desires. According to the Bhagavad Gita, the real meaning of sansaya is to give up selfish acts. The Gita does not say that sanyasa is about giving up all earthly possessions and desires.

The Sanskrit meaning of tyaga is to detach from the results of an action. In the Bhagavad Gita, Krishna specifies three types of tyaga: "Sacrifice, selfless giving, and self-discipline are three types of tyaga that should be exercised without selfish desires" (18:5). The meaning of sacrifice is the act of surrendering something; it is about paying the price today for ensuring tomorrow's success. Sacrifice is a fundamental human challenge, whether for leadership or for followership. In order to gain something, we need to expend something. Time, effort, and resources need to be sacrificed or expended to gain something in return. Organizations cannot find future success if time and effort cannot be sacrificed today.

Selfless giving is a characteristic of a true leader—a sattvic leader. Selfless giving is the act of giving for a good purpose without expecting something in return. Self-discipline becomes a form of tyaga when one has control over negative emotions and behaviors such as anger, greed, and pride. Being aware of one's emotions, controlling negative emotions, and promoting positive emotions are ways to exercise tyaga. Every human being has a propensity toward negative emotions. Renouncing this propensity is the third true meaning of tyaga.

Krishna also explains that not all renunciations are true and meaningful: "To abstain from one's responsibilities is called a deceptive or tamasic renunciation" (18:7). When leaders care less about the needs of their people, it becomes a tamasic renunciation. When leaders care only about their personal benefits and not care about the welfare of their organizations, it becomes a tamasic renunciation.

Shying away from one's responsibilities over apprehension and anxiety is not a meaningful renunciation. Krishna says, "To abstain from responsibilities because of the fear from difficulty or discomfort—it is called the rajasic renunciation" (18:8). Staying away from responsibilities because of the fear of hard work and complicated tasks is not a true renunciation. A leader who fears hard work to improve his organization is an example of rajasic renunciation.

A true renunciation is one that is undertaken with courage and without selfish attachments. By acknowledging one's responsibilities and doing everything in his or her capacity to fulfill those responsibilities, a person performs a true renunciation—a sattvic renunciation. Krishna notes, "Sattvic renunciation is to fulfill your responsibilities without selfish desires knowing that you are obligated. A sattvic person neither fears unpleasant work nor seeks a work that is unpleasant" (18:9–10). When a person truly acknowledges his responsibilities, there is no judgment of the nature of work. He does not worry about the pleasantness or unpleasantness of the nature of work.

The concept of renunciation, as defined in the Bhagavad Gita, is an important part of effective leadership. By properly utilizing leadership authority, power, and incentives and by fulfilling leadership responsibilities without selfish desires, a leader can serve as a true and an effective leader.

In chapter 18, Krishna mentions specific areas where true renunciation must be practiced, as follows:

- Renounce negative thoughts, words, and actions.

- Renounce inequality and promote equality.

- Renounce selfish desires and exercise selfless service.

- Renounce indiscipline, dishonesty, and lazy attitudes; and exercise integrity and proactive-ness.

- Renounce arrogance and ignorance, and be open-minded.

- Renounce momentary happiness that is derived from selfish, igno-rant, and arrogant behaviors. Instead, seek happiness that is long-lasting and beneficial to all.

## Causes of Actions

Renouncing negative actions requires a deeper understanding of the causes of actions. By eliminating the negative causes of actions, we can avoid neg-ative actions. Krishna identifies "five elements of actions. They are—the body, the doer, the act of doing, the ego, and the will" (18:15).

The needs of a human body are not limited solely to basic needs such as food, clothing, and shelter. The senses, which usually drive the body and its actions, desire more than just these basic needs. To see better things and not only good things, to hear better things and not only good things, to feel better things and not only good things—the senses are prone toward ambition. Ambition is not always negative; however, when ambi-tions run too high, our actions become aggressive, often unnecessary, and desperate. Therefore, finding a balance in the needs of our senses can cre-ate a balance in our actions.

The feeling of superiority also drives us to act aggressively, unnecessar-ily, and desperately. Ego-driven actions always create unfavorable situa-tions for someone involved in the interaction. When two egocentric parties interact, one or both parties are likely to lose. Ego-driven interactions do not always work best for effective leadership. Leadership becomes effective when it creates win-win results for all. Ego-driven leadership cannot create win-win results at all.

Every action is also influenced by will or determination. Bold and courageous actions require a high degree of determination. Great and effective leadership comes from leaders who have a high degree of determination. Because of their strong determination, they bring about transformations and lead their people and organizations through adversity. A strong determination on the leader's part also disseminates a sense of confidence in their organizations.

Krishna also points out the association between actions and knowledge. He says, "Knowledge, the thing to be known, and the knower—these three promote actions" (18:18). In the next section, we explore how Krishna describes knowledge.

## True Knowledge

In Krishna's words, true knowledge is sattvic knowledge. "Sattvic knowledge promotes unity and equality of all" (18:20). Sattvic knowledge teaches us the correlations between objects and beings in this world. No existence is isolated from any other existence. Sattvic knowledge is about seeing the whole instead of the smaller parts that make up the whole. This is also known as systems thinking, as discussed in chapter 11.

Understanding the dynamics of the rain cycle is a simple illustration of sattvic knowledge. The sun heats up the ocean water, and the water evaporates to become water vapor. The water vapor cools and turns into tiny droplets of water. These droplets come together to form clouds. When the clouds become heavy, the water droplets fall to the ground as precipitation. Precipitation eventually flows back to the oceans mostly through the rivers. All these events that constitute the rain cycle are distant in time and space, yet they are all connected within the same cycle. Each event influences the whole cycle, but that influence is not easily noticeable. We can only understand the rain cycle by considering the whole, not just one individual event of the cycle. The cause and effect of the rain cycle are not limited to clouds, rivers, and oceans, however. Everything that consumes water or generates water is part of that large system.

While sattvic knowledge should be promoted, there are different types of knowledge that should be renounced. "Rajasic knowledge sees segregation of things, and tamasic knowledge misunderstands one small thing and assumes it as a whole" (18:21–22). Assuming that each object or being exists in its entirety without depending on another object or being is an error. Such an assumption gives rise to isolation and division among isolated entities. Such an assumption contradicts systems thinking.

In the context of leadership, sattvic knowledge gives way to the right vision that acts as a unifying force in an organization. Therefore, sattvic knowledge helps leaders bring people and resources together for the common good. Leaders have to unite everyone and everything possible in their organizations, so unity serves to fulfill the vision and goals of their organizations.

## Meaningful Actions

Sattvic knowledge creates sattvic actions. If the knowledge is pure and righteous, that knowledge creates actions that are also pure and righteous. "A sattvic action is any action that is undertaken without selfish desires and without the fear of it being pleasant or unpleasant" (18:23). When we know that something is right and worth pursuing, we often do not fear the complexities of the actions.

Gandhi's pursuit of independence for India was a sattvic action. Dr. King's fight for civil rights of oppressed Americans was a sattvic action. Sattvic actions are not always limited to political movements. In a sattvic action, Aaron Feuerstein, CEO of Malden Mills, prioritized the well-being of his employees over other considerations in spite of the threat of a financial loss to his company.

In contrast, leaders like Albert Dunlap acted with selfish interests, with no consideration for others or the consequences of his actions. Leaders like Pol Pot and Hitler acted with extreme violence. Their actions, according to Krishna's discourses, symbolized rajasic and tamasic actions. Krishna says, "A rajasic action is an action undertaken with selfish desires and too much stress. A tamasic action is an action undertaken without thinking of the consequences, or causing injuries to others" (18:24–25).

## What Makes a Good Worker?

Sattvic actions produce sattvic work. People who perform sattvic work are sattvic workers. Krishna defined a sattvic worker as "someone who is free from ego and selfish desires. He has true conviction, so he is full of enthusiasm. He practices equanimity in adversity and prosperity" (18:26). The feelings of superiority, aggressiveness, and desperation always produce negative impacts on others. There is no room for teamwork and collaboration when there is ego or personal interests. Egotism and selfish desires are negative forces, especially for leaders striving for effectiveness.

Full of personal interests and unstable in times of adversity and prosperity—these are the characteristics of a rajasic worker. "A rajasic worker is full of selfish desires. He is overtly joyous in prosperity and overtly depressed in adversity" (18:27). Much worse is a worker who is deceitful and unaware of his responsibilities: "A tamasic worker is undisciplined, dishonest, lazy, and procrastinating" (18:28).

It is interesting to find the concept of the division of labor mentioned in the Bhagavad Gita. Krishna mentions four categories of workers—*kshyatriya, brahmin, vaishya,* and *shudra* (18:41). In the ancient East, each worker had specific job responsibilities. *Kshyatriyas* were responsible for leadership, courage, and strength (18:43). *Brahmins* were responsible for learning and teaching (18:42). *Vaishyas* were responsible for trade and commerce, and *shudras* were responsible for various services (18:44).

Although this traditional division of labor, as described in the Bhagavad Gita, blended into the social structure rather than the economy of many places in the Indian subcontinent, it is noteworthy that, in the times of the Bhagavad Gita, the division of labor was used to form the collective socio-economic structure. Thousands of years have passed since then; and this concept has been mostly misinterpreted as a social order, which has given rise to many social discrepancies. In the recent years, a new division of labor has emerged, which is based on knowledge, expertise and, individual potential. Unlike the times of the Bhagavad Gita and Mahabharata when feudalism was more prevalent, democracy has promoted opportunities that have expanded the horizons of individuals on social and economical frontiers.

It is also worth mentioning that thousands of years before Frederick W. Taylor (1856–1915) defined work and workers and Peter F. Drucker (1909–2005) defined knowledge and knowledge workers, the concepts of work and knowledge were already discussed in the Bhagavad Gita. This provides a hint that management science, as we understand it today, was a subject of great interest in the ancient East although it was explored in a more philosophical or spiritual framework.

## Virtuous Intellect

Intellect is the capacity to reason intelligently, logically, and with total awareness. When the process of reasoning is obscured by arrogance and ignorance, the level of intelligence and logic decreases. According to Krishna, this is tamasic intellect. "Tamasic intellect is driven by arrogance and ignorance toward wrong actions" (18:32). A lack of awareness deteriorates the process of reasoning. One cannot tell what is right and what is wrong. A person without awareness cannot distinguish between right and wrong actions. Krishna refers to this as rajasic intellect. "Rajasic intellect cannot distinguish between right action and wrong action and does not know when to act and when not to act" (18:31).

When a person has total awareness of the self and his surroundings and has renounced arrogance and ignorance, the true intellect prevails. The ability to reason with the highest degree of intelligence and logic and with total awareness is sattvic intellect. Krishna says, "Sattvic intellect knows when to act and when not to act, what is right action and what is wrong action, what is fear and what is courage, what is freedom and what is bondage" (18:30).

Effective leaders always act with sattvic intellect. They think without arrogance and ignorance and are always cognizant of everyone's emotions and behaviors, including their own. A simple story illustrates this kind of intellect. Once a mother brought her son to Gandhi and requested him to tell her son to give up sugar. Gandhi said, "Come back in a week." The mother and her son left with a surprised look. A week later, she came back to Gandhi. This time, Gandhi told the boy, "You must give up sugar." The mother was still very perplexed, so she asked Gandhi, "Couldn't you have told him that last week?" Gandhi smiled and responded, "No, because I hadn't given up sugar last week."[1]

## Harnessing True Determination

Courage is not possible without first renouncing fear. Trust is not possible without first renouncing deceitfulness. Knowledge and wisdom are not possible without first renouncing arrogance and ignorance. Great challenges in life require strong determination. Fear, deceitfulness, arrogance, and ignorance always bring obstacles in the way of determination. When we seek our vision and goals with open-mindedness, trust, and courage, we become more determined. According to Krishna, this type of determination is sattvic will: "Sattvic will is created by focusing on the harmony between the soul, intellect, mind, and body" (18:33). Strong determination is not possible without remaining focused on the goals. Focus helps us to align our body, mind, and spirit with our goals.

It is also true that we can develop a strong determination when we pursue things and objects of our personal desire. According to Krishna, however, such a determination is not a true determination. Such a determination is called rajasic will. "Rajasic will is created by selfish desires like the desire for wealth, reputation, and ego" (18:34). Selfish desires increase the tendency for fear, deceitfulness, arrogance, and ignorance. If a person is focused solely on personal benefits, he is more likely to use inept means to attain those benefits. When fear and deceitfulness shroud our mind, it gives way to tamasic will: "Tamasic will is created by harnessing arrogance, ignorance, fear, and dishonesty" (18:35).

## Pursuit of True Happiness

Krishna calls true happiness as sattvic happiness. Krishna's definition of sattvic happiness provides insight in today's world of instant gratification. The ancient wisdom suggests that true happiness is not instant gratification: "Sattvic happiness is the happiness that tastes like poison in the beginning, but tastes like nectar in the end" (18:37). The metaphorical meaning of poison is patience, perseverance, and hard work. True happiness cannot be attained without patience, perseverance, and hard work. No job gives more happiness than one done with time and effort. No object gives more happiness than one obtained with time and effort.

In contrast, happiness derived without time, effort, and hard work is called tamasic happiness: "Tamasic happiness is the pleasure that tastes like nectar in the beginning but tastes like poison in the end" (18:38). When we spend enough time and effort on something, we develop a sense of appreciation for ourselves and for the work we do. We get a sense of appreciation for the goals we are pursuing, and we often have a sense of a purpose in this pursuit. When we achieve objects and goals without time, effort, and hard work, the gratification is momentary. Tamasic happiness is usually sensual happiness. We misinterpret happiness perceived by our senses as true happiness. But sensual happiness is usually not long-lasting.

According to Krishna, happiness derived from indiscipline and ignorance is called rajasic happiness. Ignorance can be bliss but only until we become knowledgeable: "Rajasic happiness is drawn from activities such as ignorance, laziness, or excessive sleep. Happiness is an illusion both in the beginning and in the end" (18:39).

The pursuit of true happiness is an important issue in leadership. Whether in government, community, or business, the ultimate goal of leaders is to assist followers in their pursuit of true happiness. A national leader's goal is to make citizens happy. A community leader's goal is to make the community happy. A business leader's goal is to make customers, employees, and other stakeholders happy. When the followers' happiness is a focus of an organization's or group's leaders, that group thrives.

Is there an effective leader who has provided instant gratification for his or her followers? Many effective leaders of our times and their followers realized true happiness only after a long struggle. Gandhi and his followers struggled for more than four decades for India's independence. Mandela withstood twenty-seven years of prison to abolish apartheid. Some notable business leaders, such as Jack Welch and Louis Gerstner Jr., spent many years of hard work to improve their businesses. In the cases of effective leadership, true happiness comes after long and enduring struggles. The experience in the beginning is bitter, and the end is rewarding. This is sattvic happiness.

## From Excellence to Emancipation

Excellence is doing something at its best. Excellence is also the ability to do something at its best over and over again with consistency. When we talk about excellence in relation to leadership, leaders have to demonstrate excellence over time to be effective. There is no such thing as onetime effective leadership.

In the discourses of the Bhagavad Gita, Krishna also talks about excellence: "Excellence can be attained by dedicating to one's own obligations and responsibilities" (18:45). Effectiveness comes when one fulfills one's own responsibilities—not someone else's—with excellence.

Krishna also says, "No one should abandon obligations because they are defective. Every action is surrounded by defects just like fire is surrounded by smoke" (18:48). We should not turn away from our obligations because they are challenging or difficult. In many cases, we have a conscious choice toward our obligations unless we are forced by some authority. A leader has a conscious choice to lead negligently or to lead effectively. Because of this conscious choice, we are free within the framework of our obligations. But we should also remember that there is no freedom without fulfilling our obligations. There is no liberty without carrying out our duties. According to John Gardner, the famous American writer, teacher, and leader, "It isn't in the grand design that we can have freedom without obligation."[2]

What if we do not acknowledge our obligations? Krishna says, "The karma, which is born from your character, will drive you to do things which you may not wish to do" (18:60). Karma is the cause and effect of our actions and behaviors over time. According to the ancient Eastern wisdom, there is always a cause to every incident we encounter or every action we undertake. And every incident we encounter or every action we undertake becomes the cause of successive incidents and actions. The cause and effect of our obligations work in the same manner. We cannot disconnect ourselves from our obligations because, even if we turn away from our obligations, we will be liable to the causes and effects of not accepting them.

As John Gardner notes, true freedom is not possible without first fulfilling our obligations and responsibilities. True freedom is also not possible without striving to fulfill our responsibilities to the best of our abilities. Between attaining freedom and fulfilling responsibilities, there are certain things we must renounce. This is the ultimate challenge according to the Bhagavad Gita. "People who advance from excellence to emancipation are those who are free from selfish desires; those who have high level of emotional intelligence; those who are free from likes and dislikes; those who lead life with yoga and meditation, with control over thoughts, speech, and actions; those who are free from ego, anger, arrogance, and pride" (18:49–53). According to Krishna, these are the actions leaders must take if they truly wish to be effective.

◆    ◆    ◆

At the end of his discourses, Krishna again encourages Arjuna to rise and fight the battle of Kurukshetra. The metaphorical meaning of "battle," as discussed in the Bhagavad Gita, is not always a clash between two armies. It could be a battle between any force of good and evil. It could be a battle of ethics and morality that brews in our hearts and minds. Or, it could be a battle between the virtuous and the corrupt. In the Bhagavad Gita, Krishna advises us to accept the challenge to fight against the evil, corrupt, and sinful. Leaders have more accountability to this challenge because followers look to them for guidance. Leaders are the frame of reference for ethics and morality. We expect our leaders to have a high degree of morality and ethics; we expect our leaders to be sattvic.

## Chapter 18: Krishna's Leadership Lessons

- Leadership success is possible by practicing sacrifice, selfless giving, and self-discipline.

- A true leadership renunciation is one undertaken with courage and without selfish attachments.

- A leader performs a true renunciation—a sattvic renunciation—by acknowledging his or her responsibilities and doing everything in his or her capacity to fulfill the responsibilities.

- Leaders can harness true willpower by renouncing arrogance, ignorance, fear, and deceitfulness.

- Leaders should renounce biased knowledge. Instead, they should seek knowledge that promotes unity and equality.

- Leaders should seek true happiness that is long-lasting rather than momentary.

# Notes and References

## Introduction

1. The Bhagavad Gita mentions Bheema, Arjuna's brother, as the "protector" of the army of the Pandavas. In some translations, Bheema has also been noted as the commander. However, as the focus of the Gita is clearly on the leadership challenges Arjuna faces, it is imperative that Arjuna is the foremost leader of the army of the Pandavas.

2. Senge, Peter M. *The Fifth Discipline: The Art & Practice of the Learning Organization.* New York, NY: Currency Doubleday, 1990. 78.

3. Referenced from http://hinduism.about.com/library/weekly/extra/bl-gitacomments.htm

4. Emerson, Ralph Waldo. *Selections from Ralph Waldo Emerson: An Organic Anthology.* Boston, MA: Houghton Mifflin, 1960.

5. Referenced from *Walden—The Pond in Winter* by Henry David Thoreau.

6. Zohar, Danah. *SQ: Connecting With Our Spiritual Intelligence.* New York, NY: Bloomsbury Publishing, 2000.

## Chapter 1

1. Gerstner, Louis V. *Who Says Elephants Can't Dance? Inside IBM's Historic Turnaround.* New York, NY: HarperBusiness, 2002. 182.

## Chapter 2

1.  Goleman, Daniel et al. (December 2001). "Primal Leadership: The Hidden Driver of Great Performance." *Harvard Business Review.*

2.  Hemp, Paul et al. (December 1, 2004). "Leading Change When Business is Good: The HBR Interview—Samuel J. Palmisano." *Harvard Business Review.*

3.  Hurd, Mark and Nyberg, Lars. *The Value Factor: How Global Leaders Use Information for Growth and Competitive Advantage.* Princeton, NJ: Bloomberg Press, 2003. 88.

4.  Collins, Jim. *Good to Great: Why Some Companies Make the Leap—and Others Don't.* New York, NY: HarperBusiness, 2001. 41.

## Chapter 3

1.  Manning, George and Curtis, Kent. *The Art of Leadership.* McGraw Hill/Irwin, 2002. 67.

2.  Levin, Doron. *Behind the Wheel at Chrysler: The Iacocca Legacy.* New York, NY: Harcourt Brace, 1995.

## Chapter 4

1.  Descriptions of the persons extracted from nobelprize.org.

2.  Quotation taken from mkgandhi.org/truth/truthmk.htm.

## Chapter 5

1.  Walsh, Catherine. (December 17, 2001). "Leadership on 9/11: Morgan Stanley's Challenge." *Harvard Business School Working Knowledge.*

2.  Dutton, Jane et al. (January 2002). "Leading in Times of Trauma." *Harvard Business Review.*

3.  Read more about Ewing Marion Kauffman at kauffman.org.

4.  Goleman, Daniel et al. (December 2001). "Primal Leadership: The Hidden Driver of Great Performance." *Harvard Business Review.*

5.  Goleman, Daniel. *Emotional Intelligence: Why It Can Matter More than IQ.* New York, NY: Bantam, 1997.

6.  General note: There are several verses in chapter 5 on the divine qualities of a leader. One may question whether these qualities are limited to leaders from the past and whether today's leaders need more or different qualities than described in the chapter. We must keep in mind that the discourses in the Bhagavad Gita were intended for situational leadership and the applicability of these qualities to Arjuna's role in the battle of Kurukshetra.

## Chapter 6

1.  Dutton, Jane et al. (January 2002). "Leading in Times of Trauma." *Harvard Business Review.* 55.

2.  Mandela, Nelson. (1995). *Long Walk to Freedom: The Autobiography of Nelson Mandela.* Boston, MA: Back Bay Books, 1995. Page 496.

## Chapter 8

1.  Carter, Jimmy. *Living Faith.* New York, NY: Times Books, 1996. 27.

2.  Conlin, Michelle. (November 1, 1999). "Religion in the Workplace." *BusinessWeek.*

3.  Ibid.

4.  Jefferson, Thomas et al. *The Life and Selected Writings of Thomas Jefferson.* New York, NY: Modern Library Press, 1998. 289.

5. "Statements of Faith by US [sic] Presidents." *The Patriots' Herald.* http://patriotsherald.com/content/churchstate.php.

6. Ibid.

7. Ibid.

8. Ibid.

9. *George W. Bush—Faith in the White House.* The documentary quotes the October 12, 2000, issue of the *Maranatha Christian Journal.*

10. Conlin, Michelle. (November 1, 1999). "Religion in the Workplace." *BusinessWeek.*

11. Ibid.

## Chapter 10

1. King, Martin Luther Jr. and Carson, Clayborne. *The Autobiography of Martin Luther King Jr.* New York, NY: Warner Books, 1998. 24.

2. Senge, Peter M. *The Fifth Discipline: The Art & Practice of the Learning Organization.* New York, NY: Currency Doubleday, 1990. 3.

3. Ferrell, O. C. et al. *Business Ethics: Ethical Decision Making and Cases.* Boston, MA: Houghton Mifflin. 281–292.

## Chapter 11

1. Senge, Peter M. *The Fifth Discipline: The Art & Practice of the Learning Organization.* New York, NY: Currency Doubleday, 1990. 6.

2. Ibid., 68–69.

3. Ibid., 69.

4. Ibid., 73.

## Chapter 12

1. Baron, Robert A. and Byrne, Donn. *Social Psychology.* 10th edition. Prentice Hall India, 2003. 487.

2. Mandela, Nelson. *Long Walk to Freedom: The Autobiography of Nelson Mandela.* Boston, MA: Back Bay Books, 1995. Various sections.

3. The Web site of the African National Congress (ANC): http://www.anc.org.za

4. Goleman, Daniel. *Primal Leadership: Realizing the Power of Emotional Intelligence.* Boston, MA: Harvard Business School Press, 2002. 49.

## Chapter 13

1. Kotler, Philip and Lee, Nancy. *Corporate Social Responsibility: Doing the Most Good for Your Company and Your Cause.* Hoboken, NJ: John Wiley & Sons. 3.

## Chapter 14

1. *The American Heritage Dictionary of the English Language.* 4th Edition, 2000.

2. Manning, George and Curtis, Kent. *The Art of Leadership.* New York, NY: McGraw Hill/Irwin, 2002. 3.

3. Kouzes, James M. and Posner, Barry Z. *The Leadership Challenge.* San Francisco, CA: Jossey-Bass, 2002. 33.

## Chapter 15

1. Referenced from *Srimad Bhagavad Gita* by Swami Chinmayananda published by Central Chinmaya Mission Trust.

2. Senge, Peter M. *The Fifth Discipline: The Art & Practice of the Learning Organization.* New York, NY: Currency Doubleday, 1990. 3.

3. Ibid., 13.

4. Ibid.

5. *The American Heritage Dictionary of the English Language.* 4th Edition, 2000.

## Chapter 16

1. Manning, George and Curtis, Kent. *The Art of Leadership.*New York, NY: McGraw Hill/Irwin, 2002. 89.

2. *The American Heritage Dictionary.* 4th Edition. 2000.

3. Schiraldi, Glenn. *The Anger Management Sourcebook.* New York, NY: McGraw Hill, 2002. 3.

## Chapter 18

1. Ingram, Catherine. *In the Footsteps of Gandhi: Conversations with Spiritual Social Activists.* Berkeley, CA: Parallax Press, 2003. 173.

2. Gardner, John. *Excellence: Can We Be Equal and Excellent Too?* New York, NY: W.W. Norton & Company, 1984. 154.

# Index

165

978-0-595-37040-5
0-595-37040-3

Made in the USA